# THE DILESSI MURDERS

# THE DILESSI
# MURDERS

## Romilly Jenkins

*O stranger fair and good, in flower of youth,*
*Rest on the shore, while the strong melt in tears!*
D. Solomós

This edition published in 1998 in Great Britain by
Prion Books Limited
32-34 Gordon House Road,
London NW5 1LP

Copyright © Romilly Jenkins, 1961

Introduction © Brooks Richards

First published in 1961

ISBN 1-85375-280-0


Cover design by Bob Eames
Cover image courtesy of Michael Tsangaris collection, Athens
All other images courtesy of the Illustrated London News,
London
Printed and bound in Great Britain
by Creative Print & Design, Wales

To

Elizabeth Jenkins

# CONTENTS

# ILLUSTRATIONS

Map illustrating the route of the Brigands from the capture of the party at Pikermi on 11 April to the murders at Dilessi on 21 April 1870.

Portraits of Edward Herbert, Frederick Vyner, King George of the Hellenes and Thrasyvoulos Zaïmis.

Church at Oropós, attended by the Greek Brigands and their prisoners.

House of Mr. Skourtaniotis at Oropós where the hostages were confined.

The trial of the brigands in Athens. Colonel Theagenis giving evidence.

# INTRODUCTION:

## GREECE IN THE MODERN WORLD

It is nearly fifty years since I first lived in Greece. The country was struggling to recover from a German occupation, famine and astronomical inflation. Two civil wars had left it on the right side of the Iron Curtain, but only just.

All her northern neighbours were communist states. Old-fashioned Athenians spoke of going to "Europe" for their holidays. The pre-war holder of my job, as Press Attache at the British Embassy, was one of Greece's first Alpinists and had written the first book on the wild flowers of Attica. His wife was said to be the daughter of a Klepht.

When I went back in 1974, as Ambassador, the military junta that had ruled for seven years, the only dictatorship to be established in non-communist Europe since the War, had just collapsed under its own ineptitudes. Mr. Karamanlis had just returned from eleven years of voluntary exile to restore parliamentary democracy and to steer Greece towards membership of the European Common Market. The final folly of Brigadier Joannides, the most hard-line of the junta leaders, had been a bungled attempt to unite Cyprus with Greece by a military coup which brought the country to the edge of war with Turkey, when the Turks retaliated by occupying Northern Cyprus. But the Greek mobilisation was so chaotic that the chiefs of the armed forces threw the junta out and invited Karamanlis back - though not King Constantine.

Large crowds of students marched to the British and United States Embassies demanding we remove Turkish troops from Cyprus. But they were careful to leave the Turkish Embassy alone.

It was at that stage that a friend, long resident in Greece, lent me a copy of *The Dilessi Murders*. It dealt with a type of crisis which not infrequently confronts British diplomats in other parts of the world today, but the book's main interest to me was the light it threw on the Greece of a hundred years earlier, when the small, independent kingdom set up by the Protecting Powers, not without misgivings, was no more than forty years old. Romilly Jenkins' description of Greek brigandage and its symbiotic relationship with the Greek political world was fascinating, but it was his analysis of 'Truth and Ethnic Truth' and the closely related subject of the Great Idea (the restoration of the Byzantine Empire) that was most relevant to our understanding of the problems of the day, since that Idea had remained the central policy objective of Greece long after the events he described and the wreckage of Enosis - the union of Greece with Cyprus - its most recent manifestation, lay all around us.

I recommended the book to others, but it was out of print. I welcome the decision to republish it. I believe it will help many people to understand the distance Greece has travelled in modern times, her unresolved difficulties with Turkey and with her northern neighbour, Macedonia.

The Greek language, one of the major components of her national identity, probably has a longer unbroken history than any other survivor in the Indo-European cultural heritage.

The Greek identity is, I believe, a cultural, rather than a genetic one, though Greeks dislike any suggestion that they are not descendants of classical progenitors. But the traveller in Leigh Fermor's Mani at the southern end of the Peloponnese will discover that some of the villages with the most classical Greek names have acquired them in the present century as replacement for others of Slavonic origin. Greece has been subject to many migrations since the Dorians arrived 3000 years ago, but the Orthodox Church has proved able to transform Slavs, Vlachs and Albanians into Greek-speaking orthodox Christians within a few generations.

As a Byzantinologist, Jenkins well understood the central role of the Church in Greek thinking. Four centuries of Turkish occupation had largely insulated Greece from the intellectual currents that had swept over Western Europe since the Renaissance. The nineteenth-century Greek had inherited from his fifteenth-century Byzantine ancestor modes of thought and action which contemporary, secularised Europe could not understand at all. Like that ancestor, he lived on two levels of consciousness: there was the level of factual observed truth, on which he had to conduct his everyday existence. But there was a higher level of ideal truth on which he wished to be observed by the outside world. The factual observed truth was that the Greek kingdom was small and poor; twice as many Greeks lived outside the Kingdom as within it. Its independence hung on the protection afforded by foreign powers. But at the higher, ethnic level, educated Greeks felt it to be the heir of Byzantium. At that level, its main objective was to extend the limits of the state to embrace all areas of Greek settlement in the Near East with Constantinople as capital. Between everyday reality and this messianic objective, the Great Idea, stood not merely the Ottoman Empire but the nationalist ambitions of other Balkan peoples. The conventional military resources of the infant Greek state were, of course, nowhere near being able to tackle such an agenda on their own.

But Greek brigandage was a resource as well as a scourge. It had constituted an important element of the Greeks' military strength in the War of Independence. The Klephts, which means literally 'robber', had, on the whole, avoided incorporation into the small, Bavarian-officered regular army after independence, but they retained considerable prestige and had developed a curious, symbiotic relationship with the authorities and the Athenian political world. They were used by Greek political leaders, saddled since 1844 with unfamiliar, western-style political institutions, both for their domestic political purposes and for stirring up trouble for the Turks in unredeemed territories such as Thessaly and Crete.

Though Mr. Zaimis, the Prime Minister, maintained that brigandage had been extinguished, nobody believed him. Indeed the road system was so rudimentary that conventional policing was well-nigh impossible. It was therefore not surprising that Lord Muncaster and his friends were abducted, though they were only a few miles from the centre of Athens when it happened.

The abduction quickly acquired domestic political overtones - as is so often the case today when there are kidnappings of foreigners in places like Kashmir, Cambodia or Chechnya.

It occurred at a point when the advent of Mr Gladstone as Prime Minister profoundly affected the British reaction to the crisis. The Greek political godfathers expected Britain would humiliate Zaimis by resorting to gunboat diplomacy as Palmerston or his representatives in Athens, Sir Edmund Lyons and Sir Thomas Wyse, would have done.

But Palmerston was dead and Gladstone, a lifelong philhellene, had always deplored the bullying of small and weak governments. Erskine was left to deal with the crisis and he made a mess of it. He was, however, shockingly treated by the British Foreign Office.

It is interesting to note that British public opinion was critical of Gladstone's 'hands off' policy and felt that the country's standing had deteriorated since Palmerston's famous "Civis Romanum Sum" speech in 1850. The change of policy was not, however, permanent: we and the French rode roughshod over Greek neutrality in the First World War and the Protecting Powers did not formally renounce their right to interfere until 1923. The glaring discrepancy between Greek pretensions and realities laid open to international scrutiny and opprobri-um by the Dilessi murders, was a severe setback for the Great Idea. But, as the main element of Greek foreign policy the Idea had other major weaknesses. The rest of the world was no longer living in the Byzantine fifteenth century and the concept of a renewed Greek imperialism in the Near East was unrealistic. Secondly, although Greece had been the first of the Ottoman Empire's Balkan dependencies to break free, by 1870 all her northern neighbours had developed their own brands of national irredentism. Thirdly, Greek populations were far more widely dispersed throughout the Near East than those of the Serbs, Romanians, Bulgars and Albanians. The main concentrations of Greeks were to be found in and around Smyrna [Izmir], Lycia, Constantinople [Istanbul], Trebizond, the Pontic Alps and Cyprus, but they were separated by large Turkish populations.

The rich province of Thessaly was added to Greece by the Great Powers in 1878. This gave the kingdom a common fron-tier with Turkish-ruled Macedonia, with its proverbially mixed population of Serbs, Bulgars, Turks, Albanians and Greeks. The Turks, on the principle of divide and rule, had created a sepa-rate Bulgarian Exarchate to undermine Greek domination of the Patriarchate and its hierarchy. The Greeks attacked the Turks on this front in 1897 and suffered a humiliating defeat. They then resorted to sending bandit-like guerrilla bands into Macedonia and the Bulgarians did the same. In the Balkan Wars of 1912-13, a coalition with Serbia and Bulgaria enabled Greek forces to seize Salonika, though they only beat the Bulgarians to it by a matter of hours. The city was important to Greece's northern neighbours as the best deep-water port in the North-ern Aegean. For all its Byzantine past, in 1912 the Greeks were no more than a small minority in its cosmopolitan population: Sephardic Jews predominated – a community descended from those expelled from Spain in 1493 and still speaking fifteenth-century Castilian. They had helped the Ottoman Turks conquer the Balkans and had made the city the commercial centre for a vast hinterland. They regarded the Greeks as rivals in business and the imposition of new national frontiers across their traditional trade routes crippled the city's prosperity. The Greek Navy meanwhile had extended Athens' hold on the predominantly Greek-inhabited islands of the Aegean - to Mytilene, Chios and Samos which lie close to the shore of Asia Minor.

The First World War split the Greek political world from top to bottom. King Constantine was the Kaiser's brother-in-law, while Venizelos and his followers strongly supported Great Britain and France. With his help nine divisions took part in the final Allied breakthrough on the Salonika front in 1918. With the Ottoman Empire prostrate, Venizelos persuaded the Allies to help him land a Greek force at Smyrna, a city with more Greek inhabitants than Athens. It seemed briefly as though the Great Idea's central aim might be achieved. But Mustapha Kemal, the future Attaturk, who had humbled the Allies at Gallipoli, rallied Turkish nationalists. Fighting broke out and Kemal repudiated the Sultan's authority. At one point it looked as though the Greeks might capture the nationalists' headquarters and base at Ankara, but in 1922 the tide turned against the Greeks. Smyrna was sacked, with the loss of 30,000 Greek and Armenian lives. Venizelos was by then out of office and the Allies did no more than help the Greeks evacuate. Under the Treaty of Lausanne there was an exchange of populations: 1,100,000 Greeks left Turkey and 380,000 Turks left Greece. A high proportion of the Greek refugees from Asia Minor were resettled in Greece's northern province of Macedonia, where they formed 40% of the total population and transformed the ethnic composition of the province. Then the Nazis liquidated the Sephardic Jews of Salonika - the largest ethnic group in the city - and many Macedonian Slavs left after the defeat of the Communist forces in the second civil war.

Greece is now one of the most ethnically homogenous

states of South-East Europe – an ironic consequence of the failure of the Great Idea in Asia Minor. But the Greeks view with understandable concern any signs of Slav irredentism over Macedonia. The break-up of Yugoslavia and the consequent ethnic instability of a large part of the Balkans worries them greatly. They are too nervous to add to that instability by laying claim to the substantial Greek-speaking population of Southern Albania.

The final failure of the Great Idea was Cyprus. Greece had acquired the Dodecannese islands under the Italian Peace treaty of 1947, leaving the 80 per cent Greek population of Cyprus as the largest in the Near East outside the frontiers of the Greek state. So long as the British were the Greek government's main support against Communist insurgency Athens did little to encourage Greek Cypriot demands for Enosis - union with Greece. But when Britain yielded that role to the United States and were beginning to dismantle the Empire, the inhibition lapsed and the Papagos government expressed its interest. Unfortunately, the British reply seemed to rule out any relinquishment of sovereignty indefinitely, since the island's strategic facilities were still very-much needed. General Grivas, a Cypriot-born Greek officer was sent to the island to organise civil disobedience, backed by political violence. But the Turks then took a hand: in 1955 they inspired riots against the Greek community in Istanbul, which numbered 100,000 and had been allowed to stay on by the Lausanne settlement. There were a number of deaths and damage to property was on a massive scale. The Turks proclaimed their wish to see Cyprus partitioned, but they and the Karamanlis government in Athens eventually agreed to an independent Cyprus government and British sovereign base areas. Grivas and his supporters were bitterly disappointed by the settlement, which they attempted with Ioannides' help to overturn in 1974. The Turks still control 40 per cent of the island which they then seized and the

Greek community in Istanbul has all but disappeared. The 1974 crisis has given rise to a second unresolved dispute between Athens and Ankara - over the Aegean. Tension in the area began in 1973 under the junta when the Greeks announced the discovery of commercially exploitable quantities of oil off the island of Thasos. Turkey then claimed the right to prospect for oil in areas regarded by Greece as forming parts of her continental shelf.

This led to bellicose posturing, but the issue has now been partially defused. The chances of a major oil discovery seem in any case small, as the area has been subject to earthquakes. Another problem has arisen, however, over the heavy fortification by the Greeks of various of their Aegean islands, following the Turkish invasion of Cyprus in 1974. The Turks contend this is a breach of the Lausanne Treaty of 1923 and of the Paris Treaty of 1947, under which the islands were to remain demilitarised. The Greeks invoke the inherent right of self-defence.

These long-standing tensions all derive from Greece's past pursuit of the Great Idea. Karamanlis sought very deliberately and basically for political reasons to redirect his country's outlook away from its Balkan and Near Eastern past towards the developing European Union. His successful campaign for accelerated membership was achieved partly because the governments of Western Europe had a bad conscience about their attitudes during the anachronistic period of military rule and were concerned to give a fair chance to restored parliamentary democracy. There seemed at one point room for doubt whether Andreas Papandreou would be willing to pursue the same course, as his powerful rhetoric as opposition leader was hostile both to the EEC and NATO connection. But his belief that Greece's future lay with Assad of Syria and Gaddafi of Libya and the Third World had been tacitly laid aside before he came to power as leader of Greece's first socialist government in 1981.

The fact that the change occurred without violence meant that Greek politics is no longer over-shadowed by memories of the civil wars. Its tone may remain nationalistic, but the Great Idea has had its day.

Sir Brooks Richards
British Ambassador to Greece 1974–78
Dorset, 1998.

# THE AUTHOR

Romilly Jenkins, who died in 1969 at the age of 62, was both a classicist of great distinction, and one of the most remarkable Byzantinists of his time.

Jenkins' post-graduate studies were spent at the British school of archeology in Athens. Thereafter he lectured in Modern Greek at Cambridge University, and subsequently became Professor of Modern Greek at Kings College, London. He belonged to that rare species of scholar who comprehended the entire development of Greek civilisation from Homer to the present time. His studies of the works of the poets Solomos and Palamas are as highly regarded today as they were when they were published nearly sixty years ago.

In 1960 Jenkins turned his attention to Byzantine Studies and moved to the Dumbarton Oaks Byzantine Centre of Harvard University in Washington DC. Here he became known as the foremost living authority on the Macedonian period of the Byzantine Empire, from the ninth to the eleventh centuries. Not only was he a brilliant textual analyst, but he was able to incorporate the results of his research in books for the general public. His work Byzantium: the Imperial Centuries (1966) was very well received; and he was preparing a full-length history of the Byzantine Empire at the time of his death.

Jenkins was not afraid of controversy, and some of his views on modern Greece aroused hostility in that country. *The Dilessi Murders*, which describes in detail the hostage crisis of 1870 whose tragic outcome severely tested Anglo-Greek relations, contains in particular a chapter entitled 'Truth and Ethnic Truth' that encountered considerable Greek sensitivity.

Jenkins' life was cut short before his abilities as a scholar and a writer could find their fullest expression. But the body of work which he left amply demonstrated his many-sided talents.

Sir Michael Jenkins
London, 1998.

# FOREWORD

On the afternoon of Thursday, 21 April 1870, Edward Henry
Charles Herbert, Frederick Grantham Vyner, Edward Lloyd
and Alberto de Boÿl were murdered by brigands near the
Greek village of Dilessi, on the coast of Boeotia. The story of
these murders, together with the circumstances which led up
to and followed them, is the subject of this book. The incident
throws an interesting light both on the history of English
diplomacy and on that of the regeneration of Greece. It is also
a good tale in itself, and I have tried not to mar it in the telling.
The disaster provoked widespread alarm, anger and dismay at
the time, but these were quickly extinguished in the far greater
and more momentous tragedy of the Franco-Prussian War,
which broke out three months later. Nearly a century has gone
by since the murders took place, and in reading about them we
are removed to a world very different from our own. Only in
the bold pronouncements of Mr. Gladstone do we detect the
origins of a foreign policy which modern Britain has, for better or worse, since come to accept as a ruling principle. For the
rest, the Greece of 1870 has changed beyond recognition; and
the England of 1870 has long passed away.

The only tolerably full and connected account of the
Dilessi murders was published sixty-three years ago by the

Frenchman Watbled (Bibliography no. 41); but Watbled had no access to the most important documents of the day, and besides his account is in many respects inaccurate. This is partly due to a tendency to dramatise events which in themselves were quite sensational enough.

My account is based primarily on the English diplomatic correspondence which passed between Athens and London in the years 1870 and 1871 (Bibliography no. 15). All correspondence quoted below without further specification derives from this source. The series of Parliamentary Papers published in 1870 and 1871, under the title 'Correspondence respecting the Capture and Murder by Brigands of English and Italian Subjects in Greece' (Temperley-Penson nos. 783, 805), contains quite a full selection of the original documents, but there were of course many important omissions from it. The Greek Blue Book (Bibliography no. 18) is by comparison meagre and unhelpful. Next to the English diplomatic documents, the published collection of Frank Noel's letters (Bibliography no. 29) provides the fullest and most authentic information.

Many acknowledgements must be made. Unpublished Crown Copyright material in the Public Record Office (Bibliography no.15) has been reproduced by permission of the Controller of Her Majesty's Stationery Office; and unpublished material in the Gladstone Papers (Bibliography no. 17) by permission of Mr. C. A. Gladstone and of the Manuscript Department of the British Museum. Without the permission of these authorities my book could not have been published: and I am deeply grateful for their generosity, as well as for the courtesy and efficiency of the staffs both of the Public Record Office and of the Museum. Extracts from Austrian documents (Bibliography no.8) are printed by permission of the Haus-, Hof-, und Staatsarchiv, Wien; and were copied and most kindly put at my disposal by my friend Mrs. D. Dontas. The Directors of two Libraries in Athens, the Gennadeion (Dr. P. Topping) and the

Voulí (Dr. Provatás), gave me every facility: the former library houses an unrivalled collection of printed sources on contemporary Greek brigandage; the latter, all the important contemporary Greek newspapers. The Managing Committee of the British School of Archaeology at Athens gave permission to publish extracts from some partly unpublished writings of George Finlay (Bibliography no. 13). The Rt. Hon. Philip Noel-Baker most kindly put at my disposal some letters of Finlay to Edward and Alice Noel (Bibliography no. 14). Sherrard furnished copies of other letters of George Finlay bearing on the Dilessi Affair, identified by him in Athens; and Dr. J. K. Campbell gave me valuable information about Vlachs and Sarakatsans. Needless to say, none of these ladies or gentlemen is in any way responsible for the use I have made of materials put at my disposal. The inscription of the book to my sister Elizabeth is a small acknowledgement of the fact that without her encouragement it would not have been written, and that without her advice it would have been much worse than it is.

Dates are given throughout in the 'new style', that is to say, twelve days later than those of the 'old style' still current in Greece in 1870. On some of the Greek names an acute accent is placed, to denote a stressed syllable.

R.J.

CHAPTER ONE

# GREEK BRIGANDAGE

Master, be one of them; it's an honourable
kind of thievery.

THE TWO GENTLEMEN OF VERONA

During the latter part of the nineteenth century the state of
public order even in European countries, as well as in many
parts of the New World, was far worse than would be tolerated
today. Crime and violence walked hand in hand with poverty
through large districts of the great cities of England: in London,
and Manchester, and Sheffield. Many of their streets were
infested by foot-pads and garrotters, and were unsafe even for
male pedestrians. Still in 1870 the area about St. Giles' Circus,
mid-way between the West End and the City of London, preserved the character of a seventeenth-century Alsatia or of a
Dickensian Tom-all-Alone's. Many parts of Ireland, which was
waging its perennial, squalid war of liberation, were at the
mercy of the incendiary and the assassin. In the less-settled
countries abroad, in Hungary, Spain, Italy, Sicily and the Balkans, organised banditry was an inveterate and seemingly inerad-
icable institution: such as it must be always, where the central
government is weak, or the terrain inaccessible and mountain-
ous; and where the offender against the laws has the only too
easy recourse of taking to the hills and living by rapine and
blackmail. It is against such a background of general lawlessness
that Greek brigandage at this time must be surveyed. One
might, it is true, have had to travel far to find another country

1

where banditry was, as in Greece, directed and exploited by political managers;[1] but at least the circumstances of the state's inability to protect the life and property of the citizen, and of abduction, extortion, even murder, by outlaws, were not in themselves so very unusual to the men of ninety years ago.

There were however certain characteristics attaching to Greek brigandage which made that institution unique. Everybody knows the origins and history of the noble 'kleft', or thief. As early as the fifteenth century can be discerned, in the scanty records of the Othoman empire, the existence of bands of outlaws who infested the Greek highlands, interrupted imperial communications, preyed upon the peaceable lowlanders, and were able to cast over their violence and cruelty the enveloping mantle of patriotic resistance to the infidel oppressor. The Turks could devise no means of repressing them except by the recruitment of irregular forces of mountaineers, who were nearly as lawless as they. These forces, the so-called Armatoles, which were officered or led by Christians, were as much in sympathy with as opposed to the klefts whom they were employed to hold in check. The relations between the two elements were not dissimilar to those which had prevailed on the eastern borders of medieval Byzantium between the Akrites or frontier-guards and the local Saracen emirs. Neither paid any attention to the central government. Defections from kleft to armatole, and back again to kleft, were common enough; and this was the origin of that traditional symbiosis of brigand and gendarme in nineteenth-century Greece which provided such merriment to the satirical genius of Edmond About.[2]

The 'kleftic' manner of life became, in the course of centuries, idealised into the heroic. The 'captains' and their bands lived out of doors. They were necessarily of almost incredible hardihood, strength and resource. Their physical condition was maintained by ceaseless and strenuous exercise, in tossing the

---

[1] About, *Grèce contemporaine*, 388.
[2] *Le Roi des montagnes,* chapter 5: 'Les gendarmes'.

boulder, in running, in the hop-skip-and-jump. They were crack shots with their old-fashioned, silver-bound rifles, which they cleaned with more care than they bestowed on their persons. Their journeys, secret and swift, were made by night; and by day they lay in some remote, concealed refuge, the *liméri*, known only to the shepherds who maintained them with supplies. They could endure long periods of abstinence; but when they feasted on their stolen sheep and wine, they would revel and dance and sing their wild ballads with a simple joy in the good things of life which recalled the legendary kingdom of Saturn. Their lives were ruled by a rigid code of mutual loyalty, which was reinforced by hard necessity and by superstitions of very remote origin. Their victims were often, but by no means always, Turks. A rich Greek might also be the object of their depredations: for to be rich under an alien government was to be in sympathy with that government. For the rest, the rural population furnished them with supplies, given either willingly as to patriots, or under compulsion as to marauders. They were fierce and brutal, yet not without a certain savage nobility which appealed very strongly to the sentiment of the Romantic Age. To the Greeks of the plains the kleft seemed to unite in his person all that was most spirited and courageous in their national character. And this sympathy, which survived among the peasantry during some few decades of Greek independence, at first constituted an additional obstacle to the extirpation of brigandage: since the Greek of 1850 still remembered how his grandmother had prayed to God that her sons might be worthy to breathe the free air of the mountain-tops, and thence, with their rebel fraternity, to descend on the hated mussulman tyrant. The klefts had indeed done no small service to the Greek cause in the War of Independence. Their beau-idéal was Theodore Kolokotronis, who was born under a mountain tree in 1770, of a father who had once been a captain of armatoles in the district of Corinth.

In 1829 the European Powers, not without misgiving, had decided to liberate a part of Greece from the Othomans; and the establishment of the Greek kingdom under Otho of Bavaria followed in 1832. Yet the lawlessness and prestige of the kleftic life remained powerful attractions to the adventurous. What had traditionally been regarded as the justification for the kleft's life of rapine, his intolerance of a foreign yoke, could now no longer be pleaded. Yet an alternative to the Othoman oppression was soon found in the Othonian. A wide gulf opened between the centralising government at Athens, with its Bavarian henchmen and its westernised manners, and the men of the hills, who maintained that their revolt was now in defence of the old Hellenic tradition against the injustice of an alien, if legal, administration. The number of bandits in the country showed no diminution. Their ranks were constantly recruited from those who were guilty of murder, or liable for military service, or oppressed by debt, or simply attracted by a life of outlawry and easy profits. It is true that after 1832 these banditti were in official parlance no longer dignified by the name of 'klefts'. They were re-christened 'listaí'. Instead of 'thieves' they became 'bandits'. But that was, for practical purposes, the extent of the distinction. The manner of their life and operation, their consciousness of the pride of their calling, their code of laws, their depredations and their brutalities, remained the same. Until 1870 a large proportion of the country-folk regarded them, with good reason, as the lineal successors of the klefts of old, and paid them a pathetic tribute of terror and admiration.

The government of King Otho was rapidly forced to realise that brigandage, hallowed by tradition and fostered by the unquiet state of the country, could not be exterminated; and it almost as rapidly concluded that an evil which could not be helped might nonetheless be turned to useful account.

The northern frontier of the tiny kingdom ran at that time

from the Gulf of Arta to the Gulf of Volo, across the impenetrable glens and spurs of Pindus and Othrys. To patrol this frontier efficiently would have puzzled a modern 'People's Democracy', with all its apparatus of barbed wire, land-mines and
tracker dogs. It was altogether beyond the Othoman power, let
alone the much smaller power of Greece. Bands of outlaws
passed freely between Turkey and Greece, as pressure on either
side might dictate. And in the Turkish village of Kaïtza, near the
border, was established something like a rest and rehabilitation
camp for Greek or Vlach brigands, who there recruited their
powers for next season's forays beyond the frontier.

Yet, despite all the natural advantages enjoyed by the outlaws, more might probably have been done to put an end to
what had during many centuries been a national honour, but
was now become a national disgrace, had there not persisted in
King Otho's time a cleavage of interest in the ranks of Greek
society itself: that is to say, between the 'kapellophóroi' or hat-
wearers of Athens and the 'phoustanellophóroi' or kilted chieftains in the more remote parts of the kingdom. Powerful chiefs
such as Theodore Grivas or Hadji-Petros or Kriezotis were virtually independent of the central authority, and were, not
unnaturally, confounded by foreign observers with the humbler
and more dedicated brigands themselves, whom they often
maintained and often accepted into their own service as retain-
ers.[1] The state of affairs prevailing in the northern provinces of
Greece, and especially in the province of Acarnania, has frequently, and with much justice, been compared to that of the
Highlands of Scotland before 1745. In both, the wild and inaccessible nature of the country, and the absence of any roads
above the dignity of a bridle-path, rendered impossible a steady
control by the lawful government. In both, the substance of
power was in the hands of patriarchal chieftains, inordinately
conceited and supremely contemptuous of the laws and com-

[1] Finlay VII, 157– 167.

mands of their nominal sovereign. In both, the highland man's dress was a kilt which marked him off from the 'civilised' Saxon or Frank to the south of him. In both, the practice of robbery was regarded as an honorable way of life, and one which, until very recently, had been almost synonymous with patriotic warfare against the Saxon or Turkish oppressor. Even the racial and linguistic differences which divided the Gael from the Sassenach were not without their parallel in nineteenth-century Greece, though these differences were not so absolute. Many of the Greek chieftains were of what might pass for Hellenic descent, and on the other hand much of the population of Athens and other towns was of Wallachian or Albanian extraction. Nonetheless, the Albanian language might be heard with greater frequency in the north. And in any case the whole way of life in the wild tracts of Acarnania, where, as Colonel Koronaios noted in 1869, there was scarcely a church or a priest to be found, was in complete contrast to that of the quick-witted Athenian, who sported his tall hat, recited and imitated French verses, thundered in the newspapers, and jockeyed for a lucrative place or a seat in the House of Representatives.

The governments of seventeenth-century England, who had neither the means nor the strength to break down and reform the highland society, were forced to humour it, and to get such support as they could for themselves by favouring now this, now that among the more powerful chiefs. In much the same way King Otho was compelled to make use of a system which he certainly would not have chosen, but which he was unable to repress. He alternately flattered and quarrelled with the great Theodore Grivas, who exercised a despotic power over his immense estates about Vonitsa in the western highlands. And he made use of the private army of outlaws and armatoles maintained by Grivas in order to further the national policy of raiding and disturbing the Turkish provinces across the border. Many atrocious crimes had been brought home to

ated terms by Edmond About in his novel *Le Roi des montagnes:* and whatever else in that book may be fiction, the tale of brutalities committed by the gang of Hadgi-Stavros is description of incontrovertible fact.

It was recognised that such bands could not maintain themselves by political activities only, which were the least lucrative parts of their trade. They levied blackmail on every considerable landowner; but the chief part of their wealth came from abduction, extortion and wholesale plunder. It was essential to the brigands that it should be universally known that they were not to be trifled with. When they invaded a village, the first step was to bring to the boil a large cauldron of oil, by means of which the men, and even more the women, of the village were to be induced to reveal the hiding holes of treasure. Ransoms were extorted to the last farthing by threats of mutilations, many of them too revolting for description, followed by decapitation: and these threats were no idle talk. For these and similar crimes scarcely anybody was ever punished. If captured, the brigand secured, through lavish bribery on the part of his civil patron, either a formal acquittal or else a speedy escape from justice. The royal prerogative of amnesty for those convicted of criminal offences was frequently invoked in his favour by King Otho himself. In such circumstances the forces of order were hamstrung. The gendarme passed freely back and forth, into the service of brigandage and into that of the state. And, if the patron of the gang to which he adhered were in office, he might be considered as much of a state servant in the one as in the other of his functions.

To the ambiguous conduct of the armed forces must be added, as a contributory factor in the spread and impunity of brigandage, the understandable reluctance of the rural population to combine or inform against it. On the one hand, any peasant even suspected of laying an information was mercilessly persecuted by the bands, and he was lucky if he escaped with the loss of his ears and his nose and the destruction of all his property. The government could not protect him from such reprisals. On the other hand, a punitive incursion of the military into his area was attended by depredations more thorough and widespread than any inflicted by the brigands themselves. The troops lived at free quarter. They billeted themselves on him, slaughtered his fowls and animals, and swilled his wine[1]. His village, when at last they left it, presented the appearance of having been occupied by a hostile, rather than by a friendly, army. If he protested, he was likely to be taken up on a charge of complicity with brigands and carried off to Athens, where he might languish in the Mendresé prison during months and even years without trial. No peasant, unless he were a Vlach shepherd, could be found to welcome the presence of brigands in his district; yet assuredly very small encouragement was given him to do even the little that was in his power to oppose them. He was between the upper and the nether mill-stone. Agriculture in these circumstances made little progress; and it is not surprising that the historian George Finlay noted with dismay that 'the brave peasantry who formed the nation's strength grows neither richer nor more numerous'[2].

Brigandage was endemic in Greece throughout the reign of Otho (1832–62). Yet it is possible to distinguish periods when it was especially prevalent, and periods when it was relatively quiescent. The administration of Kolettis (1844–47) brought about a notable revival of its activities. It burst out again in unexampled excesses between the years 1854 and 1857. The gaols were emptied of all malefactors, who were sent *en masse* across the frontier to support the 'spontaneous uprising' of the Christian subjects of the Porte. The Anglo-French occupation of the Piraeus followed this disastrous enterprise, and in the unsettled months which ensued brigandage infested

---

[1] Finlay, AG 1870, 13 January.
[2] Finlay VII, 182.

Attica and even the route between the capital and her port. Once again a political motive was discernible: for the Court and the opposition parties were concerned to represent this outburst as a symptom of popular resistance to the invaders. During these years (1855–56) took place two celebrated plunderings, the victims of which were both connected with this history: Mr. Edward Noel's property at Achmetaga, in the island of Euboea, was ransacked; and the daughter of Mr. Boudouris was abducted from her father's mansion at Chalkis.

Some restoration of order was again seen in the years 1857–61, partly owing to the more settled conditions which followed the Anglo-French withdrawal from Piraeus, and partly, it must be said, owing to the publication in 1857 of young M. About's novel, *Le Roi des montagnes*. In this charming tale, the botanist Schultz, in company with two English ladies, falls into the hands of the brigand chief Hadgi-Stavros, the so-called King of the Mountains, and of his god-son Pericles, a captain of gendarmerie, who are of course working in the closest collaboration. In France, and elsewhere in Europe, the book enjoyed great popularity as amusing fiction. But the Greeks were galled to the quick by it and, says Grenier,[1] 'avenged the pleasantries of its author on the heroes of his romance.'

It was unfortunate for liberated Greece that the one foreign writer of genius to describe her during the nineteenth century should have been the most inveterate of her enemies. About, in 1852, had been one of the first students to visit the newly founded French Institute at Athens. From the first he had taken a jaundiced view of Athenian life and manners. Lord Byron in 1823 had observed of George Finlay that 'he seemed to have come to Greece with only a very moderate dose of enthusiasm'[2]; and the same was true of About. Nothing could please him in what he saw; and almost everything he saw

[1] Grenier, 77.
[2] Finlay, AG 1872, 14 May.

appealed to the strongest element in his nature, a morbidly keen sense of the ludicrous. He possessed also literary talents of a high order: a style both luminous and terse, and a sense of propriety which never allowed him to degenerate from satire into invective. The Greeks, who smarted under his lash, sneered at him as the 'hunchback jester', and were eager to discover or invent the motives of his dislike. John Gennadios published a story that About had been flogged by a Greek in punishment for improper advances made by him to a respectable and modest young female. The thoughtful reader will, however, probably discover more reasons than one for dismissing this tale as apocryphal.

About's first appraisal of Greek society had appeared in 1854, with the title *La Grèce contemporaine*. The book was in fact not wholly pejorative. About did justice to Greek patriotism, intelligence and desire for enlightenment. But he laid emphasis on whatever instances could be construed as ungrateful, boorish, base, cowardly, greedy and corrupt; and, in so doing, although little or nothing of what he said could be controverted, he contrived to paint, under the guise of sober and factual description, a picture as partial and satirical as that presented of English society by Gulliver to the king of Brobdingnag.

His book aroused a storm of indignation among the polite of Athens, who were his principal butt. Greece was, it is true, not the only object of his rancour. He disliked England almost as much as he disliked Greece. But whereas Englishmen cared less than nothing what About or any other foreigner might say of them, Greeks cared very much indeed. In their view Frenchmen stood next, though to be sure at a great distance, to Greeks themselves. In so far as western culture had any contribution to make to Hellenism, that contribution was to be offered by France. Greek literature, such as it was in the 1850s, owed far more to contemporary French literature than to any other. To discover that a Frenchman had found their civilisation contemptible, and had, with all the acumen of French intelligence and all the incisiveness of French expression, so mercilessly exposed it, was mortifying in the highest degree. In reply to their invectives About published his little classic on Greek brigandage, *Le Roi des montagnes*, three years later.

His brilliant and comical story was an instant success. It is still widely read as a French text-book: and English schoolboys who know nothing of Modern Greece know all about Schultz and Mary-Ann, Harris and Lobster, the fantastical Pericles and the ogre Hadgi-Stavros. The tale is told with such skill and facility that it is nearly impossible to say where truth ends and fancy begins. But that the general account of brigandage – with its tentacles spreading throughout the armed forces and society, with its enormous apparatus of corruption, and with its hideous cruelties – was an accurate one, admits of no doubt at all. At least half a dozen brigand chiefs of King Otho's time might have sat for the portrait of Hadgi-Stavros. Yet it is probable that the general effect of the novel in Europe was harmful rather than salutary. Its success was too complete. It presented a state of society so preposterous that, as the gendarme Pericles told Schultz, nobody but a Greek could take it seriously: and, in laughing till they cried at the antics of Pericles and Hadgi-Stavros, men forgot the very real tyranny and the blackmail, the tortures and mutilations, which were the order of the day in that lovely countryside.

And, after all, the respite which *Le Roi des montagnes* helped to provide was but of short duration. The flight of King Otho in October 1862 led to a year's interregnum during which the state of the country was the most miserable she had known since 1828. Law and order, both within and without the capital, were openly defied. The soldiers were out of hand. Brigand bands were recruited to capacity; and each brigand was convinced that whatever or however many crimes he committed in that halcyon twelvemonth must be wiped out by a wholesale amnesty on the arrival of the new king, George of Denmark. At this time brigands were employed by political leaders with a shamelessness and cynicism which stultified all subsequent denials that these miscreants served a political purpose, and were even a political necessity.[1] The conduct of the party chief Dimitrios Bulgaris during the October Revolution of 1862, in recruiting the band of Kyriakos, whom he later pensioned, to menace the capital itself in Bulgaris' interest, became notorious beyond the borders of Greece[2]; and such manoeuvres were by no means abandoned either by him or by his rival Mr. Koumoundouros in the years which followed the introduction of the new Constitution (1864).

In the years 1867–70 the brigand industry reached a mark higher than any previously recorded. The proximate cause of this revival was the outbreak of the Cretan revolt against the Turks. As in 1854, the Greek government had recourse to the forces of outlawry and brigandage to bolster the national cause. In 1867 the prime minister, Mr. Koumoundouros, convened an assembly of brigands in the hills of the north, and sent his war minister, D. Botzaris, to treat with them. They were offered an amnesty and a free passage to Crete in the Greek ship *Omonoia*. They were promised rich pickings in the island they were to liberate. One hundred of them accepted the offer. After several months of campaigning and plunder of friend and foe, they were rounded up by the Turks and shipped back to Greece. On their way thither, they put in at Syra; and the Greek mayor implored the Turkish naval commander, Hobart Pasha, not to allow these heroes to set foot on Syran soil. Once back in Greece, they naturally returned to the mountains, with hearts yet more mistrustful of the Athens government. 'You sent us to Crete,' said one of them to a government representative, 'you promised us many things. We came back empty-handed, and are obliged to take to brigandage again to live.'[3]

[1] Aspréas II, 15.
[2] See below, p.176; and on these events in general, Kyriakidis II, 191 ff.
[3] Noel, *Letters,* 52.

By 1870 things had not improved: if anything, they were worse than before. The government of Mr. Zaïmis, then in office, repeatedly declared that owing to their exertions brigandage had at last been finally exterminated, but nobody inside the country made the least pretence of believing it. The large majority of instances of brigandage were never reported in any of the seventy-odd newspapers then appearing in Greece, which were too busy slandering their political opponents to find space for such trivialities. According to the computation of the foreign minister, Mr. Spyridon Valaoritis, a minimum of one hundred and nine separate cases occurred between January 1869 and June 1870. Every traveller who emerged from the capital did so at his own risk; and that so many should have regarded this risk so lightly is a puzzling feature of the situation. For although most of the minor cases were concealed from public knowledge, evidence of the dangers attaching to abduction and captivity was assuredly not wanting for any Greek or foreigner who cared to look at it.

A celebrated instance, involving foreigners of high rank, had occurred in 1865. On 8 December three English travellers, Lord John Hervey, brother of the Marquess of Bristol, the Hon. Henry Strutt, son of Lord Belper, and their friend, Mr. Coore, crossed in a yacht from Patras to Dragomesti, to shoot red deer. They had been given the usual assurances that the area was free of brigands. On their return to Dragomesti in the afternoon, they were surprised by eight brigands under the redoubtable 'captain' Spyro Dellis. They were relieved of their valuables, and their yacht was boarded and plundered. Captain Dellis then had a letter written to Mr. Wood, the English vice-consul at Patras, saying that a ransom of £1,000 in English gold for each prisoner was required within eight days, and that all pursuit of the band must meantime be intermitted. Coore, as the youngest and most active, elected to stay with the brigands as hostage. Hervey and Strutt were permitted to sail back with the terms to Patras. The party was on this occasion fortunate. Mr. Wood and his brother-in-law Mr. Crowe, well understanding the serious nature of the case, made extraordinary efforts to raise the sum from their own resources and those of the English residents. An English sloop, the *Chanticleer,* happened to be in Patras roads, and her gold was added to the fund. Within the period allowed the *Chanticleer* had crossed the gulf, found the band, delivered the money and rescued the prisoner. Meantime, Mr. Coore had suffered the usual hardships and anxieties. His captors were continually on the move. His life was in danger at every alarm. On one occasion a file of militia passed nearly within touching distance of his place of concealment. His health and spirits stood him in good stead, and he was set free none the worse. But this was certainly more by good luck than good management. The Greek government was sufficiently roused by this exploit to proclaim the gang of Dellis and to put a price on their heads. But no serious attempt was made to take them; and they were so much incensed even at this show of resolution against them that they roundly swore they would have the war minister, D. Grivas, expelled from the government!

A curious feature of the affair was the part played in it by the newly appointed English Minister in Athens, the Hon. E. M. Erskine. The outgoing government of Mr. Deligeorgis had undertaken to suspend pursuit of Dellis until the prisoner Coore was safe. Yet pursuit had on two occasions nearly cost him his life. This was perfectly known to Erskine: and how one who, only four years before, had had practical experience of the dangers of calling out the military in such cases, should have been induced in 1870, under any safeguards whatsoever, to sanction it, is—to say the least—difficult to understand.

But the abduction of Mr. Sotiris Sotiropoulos, in the summer of 1866, was for many reasons the most notorious of those which took place between 1864 and 1870. In the first place, Mr. Sotiropoulos was a politician of note, an adherent of the parties first of Admiral Kanaris and later of Mr. Koumoundouros. He had been minister of finance in four short-lived administrations during the years 1864 and 1865. His misfortune therefore aroused much comment, not only in the Greek, but also in the European press; and the fact that a politician had been abducted, and his life repeatedly endangered, at a time when his political opponents were in office gave rise to many disquieting reflexions which he himself afterwards very outspokenly expressed. In the next place, his estate, from which he was carried off, lay in one of the most peaceable parts of the Morea, where brigandage had until that time been almost unknown. Finally, on his liberation, Mr. Sotiropoulos at once wrote and printed a full account of every circumstance of his own captivity and of the difficulties experienced by his relations in collecting and delivering the very large sum of gold demanded for his release This excellent little book, *Thirty-six days of Captivity and Consort with Brigands,* gave for the first time in print an authentic description of the laws, manners, beliefs and prejudices of Greek brigands; and was, as it deserved to be, extremely popular. An English version of it was published in two volumes in 1868 by a clergyman, the Rev. Mr. Bagdon, under the title *The Brigands of the Morea,* which claimed to be Mr. Sotiropoulos' narrative *chiefly* translated from the Greek. Creditable as Mr. Bagdon's performance was, it should however be used with great caution: not only is it disfigured by many errors arising from ignorance of Greek terminology, but it also contains a large number of passages which the author has inserted on his own account, without giving the smallest indication that he has ceased to translate and is beginning to compose. Nonetheless, this version was widely read by Englishmen both in England and Greece; and it is very surprising that more reference should not have been made to the valuable information contained in it during the tragic months of April and May two years afterwards.

17

Mr. Sotiropoulos was the owner of a currant-growing estate of some thirty acres at Agrili, which lies on the western coast of the Peloponnesos, a few miles south of Kyparissia. Shortly after sundown on the evening of Thursday, 9 August 1866, a gang of filthy looking ruffians invaded his property, announced their intention of abducting him for ransom, put him on a horse and led him off with all haste along the road towards Kyparissia. For the best part of a week they hurried northwards, travelling by night and lying hidden by day. They struck inland at the pass of Kleidi, and on the 12th of August they crossed the Alpheus river near Krestena. Thence they made their way to the banks of the Erymanthus, which divides the province of Elis from the Arcadian province of Gortynia. Here they remained hidden during several days, while the authorities, stimulated by popular clamour to a most unwonted and, as it proved, a most unwise display of energy, repeatedly hindered the attempts of Mr. Sotiropoulos' relations to hand over to his captors the £2,000 in gold coin which they had painfully collected. The captive was thuse placed in mortal danger. But the brigands were mercifully convinced of the sincerity of his negotiators and, instead of cutting his throat, decided to withdraw him to a more remote hiding-place until the authorities could be eluded and the transaction completed. They accordingly crossed the Erymanthus and Ladon rivers, and for five toilsome days dragged their captive on foot uphill into the mountains of Langadia, above Dimitsana in central Arcadia. Here they were on their own ground. The local shepherds, whether through interest or terror, were their allies, and furnished them with ample supplies of bread, meat and wine. A further ten days were still to elapse before the emissaries of the gang returned with the spoil. At length, on Friday, 14 September, after thirty-six days of captivity, Satiropoulos was turned loose on the western slope of Langadia and stumbled into the hamlet of Palumba, his face burnt black with exposure and covered with a month's growth of beard, his clothes unspeakably filthy and tattered, his body crawling with lice and deeply scored with the weals of his finger-nails, his nervous system cruelly deranged and all his worldly fortune lost.

He had early discovered that the chief of his captors was the notorious bandit Mitsos Laphazanis, who had served under the yet more celebrated chiefs Kitsos Nyphitsas and 'Grandpapa' Lygos. Laphazanis claimed to have been driven to brigandage to escape the hands of justice for a murder which he had committed on one who had wronged him. He had, with other brigands, aided the rebels in their revolt against King Otho in 1862. He was now the chief of a gang of ten, who lived by kidnapping and ransom.

A second and more youthful practitioner, who was to be the prisoner's chief warder, was the Vlach Thymios Karankouris. He had been bred a butcher, and thereafter had served as a constable at Athens; and although he too claimed that his wrongs had driven him to his present calling, yet he regretted his past life 'in the world' and longed only to return to it. It is to be remarked that in no member of this gang was there the smallest sign of the pride, dignity or joy in freedom of the traditional brigand. They expressed nothing but jealousy and dissatisfaction. They were stinking, verminous fugitives, abject, greedy, resentful and, apparently, very simple hearted.

True to their habits and interest, the brigands treated Mr. Sotiropoulos with as much humanity as circumstances permitted. Though they told him frankly and often that unless every penny of his ransom were paid, he had no hope of survival, yet they did what they could to alleviate his distresses in the meantime. They shared their coarse fare with him. They stole a fowl for him. They rolled him cigarettes. They carried him across rivers on their backs; played cards with him; and even undertook, at great personal inconvenience, to procure him a copy of the Gospels. But his discomfort was extreme. He was, fortunately, a man still in the prime of life; but his civilian habits had not fitted him for the rigours of such a journey as this. By day he was parched by the sun and tormented by thirst. By night he was chilled through and through and often soaked with rain. He had no change of clothes and was seldom able to wash himself, so that during most of his captivity he was as ragged and verminous as his captors. The fatigues of his enforced marches told heavily on him. Hour after hour he was hurried on over stony tracks and up mountain-sides, until his lungs were ready to burst and his clothing was drenched with sweat. These were the moments of his greatest danger: for his survival depended upon his being able to keep pace with his companions, who were tireless and inexorable. At length he gasped out, 'I cannot follow', and stood still. 'Living or dead,' replied his terrible escort, 'up we shall carry you. So get on with you, for we are in danger of being left behind.'

We have recorded the experience of Mr. Sotiropoulos at some length because, although it conformed in every detail to those of others, both Greek and foreign, who were similarly abducted, yet his published account of it drew wide attention to two aspects of brigandage which had not till then been so fully or clearly put before the public. The first of these was the system or code of laws embraced by the regular *listés*; and the second was the attitude of the Athens government to brigandage and its exploits.

The article in the brigand code of laws which was of most vital interest is thus formulated by Sotiropoulos:

When the brigands capture a prisoner with the object of getting a ransom for him, they are concerned that the prisoner's relations, and all the community, should be convinced that unless this ransom is paid, he cannot survive; and if in the meantime they encounter detachments of the military and realize that they cannot carry the prisoner off with them, their own interest demands that they should kill him; because, if they acted otherwise and thus allowed the hope that by their pursuit prisoners could be delivered without ransom, then pursuit of those with a prisoner in their hands would be intensified, and their tracking down and destruction would be certain. They have therefore consecrated as an inviolable principle, and written it into their Laws, that they must inevitably put the prisoner to death as soon as they see that they cannot retain him alive. They regard it as a great disgrace for a prisoner to escape alive out of their hands; and brigands who suffer this dishonour, forfeit their reputation and cannot find a place in any brigand organization.[1]

Secondly, it is plain from many passages in his account that Sotiropoulos believed his abduction to have been carried out at the instigation of political enemies, with a view to his ruin if not to his eventual murder. His captors, he found, had been given a much inflated estimate of his worldly goods. They stated that they were constantly receiving promises of rewards larger than any that could be got from him if they would put him out of the way. Despite every entreaty, the government of Mr. Dimitrios Bulgaris, then in office, and their local officials in Western Peloponnese, continued to pursue the gang and to impede the delivery of the ransom, a course which must sooner or later end in Sotiropoulos' death. At length even government newspapers began to hint scandal. And Sotiropoulos himself had a dream about a certain Dimitrios which needs no Freudian analyst to interpret.

One day he overheard a conversation which illustrated very painfully the opinion of the countryfolk about the Athenian politicians and their brigands. A cooper was hailed by his captors, and having readily sworn to keep their secret, began to talk to them of recent events. 'I heard the other day,' he said, 'that a Frank [he meant, a Greek politician] was found hanging headless on a tree. Well—he asked for it and, to tell you the truth, nobody was really sorry for him: he was in public life for

[1] *Thirty-six days*, 116.

21

donkey's years, and never thought of getting an amnesty granted, so as to free the world from outlaws . . . The fact is, mates,
that these bosses want the outlaws to go on, in order to intim-
idate people with them at the elections, and get their own way.
Don't you remember what Petimezás' gang did at the Philia
election last year?'

The suspicions of Mr. Sotiropoulos that his abduction was
no chance affair were later amply confirmed. The mayor of
Thelpusa, K. Kafetzís, who had been most active in pressing the
pursuit of Laphazanis, was subsequently sent to the assizes on a
charge of complicity in the abduction itself. He would, in the
opinion of the prosecutor, Mr. Doukakis, certainly have been
convicted if Sotiropoulos had appeared against him. But
Sotiropoulos, though summoned, was afraid to say what he
knew, and discreetly absented himself.[1]

All this and much more to the like effect had been common knowledge during several years before 1870. Yet responsible people, especially the English minister Erskine, seemed
curiously reluctant to be convinced of simple truths which
were based on the plainest and most irrefragable evidence.
Coore and Sotiropoulos had, it was true, not been murdered;
but it should have been clear from their own testimonies that
nothing but a phenomenal run of luck had saved them. Englishmen persisted in the notion that to be taken by brigands
was more of a lark than anything else. One lived for a few days
or weeks on fresh meat in bracing mountain air, surrounded by
courteous and picturesque ruffians: one's friends collected and
handed over a bagful of guineas: and one came back quite
stout, with all the cobwebs blown away and a story to dine out
on for the next ten years. Those who entertained this frivolous
opinion were in for a rude awakening. Something like the
Dilessi Affair was bound to happen sooner or later. Unhappily
for Greece and England it happened in the worst possible cir-

[1] Erskine to Granville, 9 August 1870.

cumstances for each of them. The result was perhaps in the long run salutary. But the price to be paid, in human life, in sorrow and in shame, was heavy beyond reckoning.

# CHAPTER TWO

# THE CAPTURE

I will advise you where to plant yourselves;
Acquaint you with the perfect spy o' th' time,
The moment on 't, for 't must be done tonight,
And something from the palace.

MACBETH

On Thursday, 7 April 1870, three English tourists of distinction
arrived at the Piraeus, and were driven up to the Hotel
d'Angleterre in Athens. The Hotel d'Angleterre, one of the
three good hotels in the city, stood then, as it stands now, on the
south side of the Constitution Square, at the corner of Hermes
Street and facing the Royal Palace, a large, ugly building erected thirty years before at vast expense by King Otho. The hotel,
though draughty and bitterly cold in winter, was spacious and
well provisioned. Its capable manager was Polyzoïs Pikopoulos,
known affectionately to many of his English guests as 'Polly'. Its
dragoman, or *valet de place*, Alexander Anemoyiannis, who conducted parties on longer or shorter excursions into the interi-
or, had also a wide, if somewhat dubious, reputation among
foreign travellers.

The three visitors, so soon to acquire universal and melancholy celebrity, were Lord and Lady Muncaster and their
young friend Frederick Vyner. Josslyn Francis, fifth Baron
Muncaster in the Peerage of Ireland, was thirty-six years old.
He had been educated at Eton, had entered the army, and
served in the Crimea, with a gallantry which had won him an
English and a Turkish decoration. His wife, whom he had married seven years before, was Constance Ann, a niece of Richard,

25

ninth Earl of Scarborough. Frederick Grantham Vyner was a boy of twenty-three. He was the youngest child of the late Colonel Henry Vyner and his wife Lady Mary. His family, though not ennobled, was a good deal older than most of the noble families of England, for its origins were to be traced at least a century before the Norman Conquest. It was also related by marriage to the most powerful families of the Whig aristocracy. Lady Mary was a daughter of Thomas Philip, Earl de Grey. Of her two daughters, the elder had married her distant cousin George Frederick Samuel, Earl de Grey and Ripon, son of the 'transient and embarrassed phantom' Goody Goderich; the younger was the wife of Charles, fourth Marquess of Northampton. Their cousin was Francis Thomas, seventh Earl Cowper, grandson of Lady Palmerston.

Next day, 8 April, the three travellers called at the English Legation, which was then in Stadium Street, and made the acquaintance of the English minister, the Hon. Edward Morris Erskine, and of his charming third secretary, Edward Herbert, a young man of thirty-two, whose only barrier to a brilliant career in diplomacy or politics was indifferent health. Herbert himself was highly connected, since he was first, and dearly loved, cousin of Henry Howard Molyneux, fourth Earl of Carnarvon. It should be added that these aristocratic connexions of Herbert and Vyner were not their only titles to consideration. Each was nearly related to a figure of prime importance in the political life of England. Herbert's cousin, Carnarvon, had been Mr. Disraeli's Minister for Colonies in 1868; Vyner's brother-in-law de Grey was Lord President of the Council in Mr. Gladstone's administration, which was then in office.

Herbert proposed that a party should be made up to visit the historic battlefield of Marathon. He extended the invitation also to his friend, Count Alberto de Boÿl, a young Piedmontese nobleman then serving as secretary of the Italian Legation;

and to Edward Lloyd, an English barrister then resident in Athens and active in the affairs of the Piraeus Railway Company. The Muncasters fell in with the proposal, and the excursion was provisionally fixed for the following Monday, 11 April. As certain arrangements had to be made, and formalities to be gone through, before the engagement could be definite, Lord Muncaster was, as late as Sunday morning, 10 April, still not quite certain that they were to go. However, all was apparently in order; and at last, go they did.

The countryside, even in Attica, was still notoriously unsafe for travellers. It was within the knowledge of the government that a powerful band of brigands had been at large since February in the Megarid; however, during the last days of March they had published a categorical statement that, owing to their exertions, Attica at least, if not the whole kingdom, was cleared of the menace. This statement was wholly delusory, and was distrusted even by Erskine.[1] Nonetheless, the authorities acted on the supposition that it was to be relied upon; and when, on Saturday, 9 April, and again on Sunday the 10th, Herbert sent the Legation's interpreter, Mr. Lambros, to give notice to the police of the intended excursion, he met with no demur and received a promise that a token escort of four mounted gendarmes should be at the party's disposal.

By midday on Sunday, therefore, the plan to go on the morrow was fixed. The preparations were entrusted to the hotel-keeper Polyzoïs and the dragoman Alexander. The best carriage road from Athens to Marathon at that time skirted, at some distance, the southern slopes of Mount Pentelicus, and then turned northward near Raphina towards the coastal plain on which the memorable engagement had been fought. With a change of carriage-horses halfway, the distance might be covered in six hours, or in twelve hours' driving there and back. The half-way post for changing horses was the hamlet of Pas-

[1] Erskine to Clarendon, 31 March 1870; Townshend 158.

sades, a mile south of the village of Pikermi. The spare horses were sent out from Athens with their grooms at four in the morning. These arrived at Passades at about seven o'clock, and waited for the carriages which would come up there about eight-thirty. On the return journey the same procedure was followed: the original pairs were harnessed in again, and the spares jogged home at leisure. This regular procedure was of course known to everybody in Attica.

At three o'clock on Sunday afternoon Alexander got into touch with a liveryman named Sayandas. He ordered him to supply two carriages at the door of the Hotel d'Angleterre at five-thirty next morning, and of course to send out the necessary two spare pairs of horses an hour or two earlier. When Alexander was afterwards asked, why he had not engaged the Maltese jobber Nicola, who was usually employed by the hotel on such occasions, he replied that he had thought Sayandas' nags more capable of the long route to be traversed.

Meanwhile, the police authorities in Athens, though they had given no hint of any further action on their part to Mr. Lambros, thought it wise that intelligence of the excursion should be communicated to the rural militia or 'flying-column' at Kephissia, whose commander, Captain Tournavitis, was instructed to patrol the road along which the party would be travelling. Tournavitis received this instruction from his superior in Athens at midnight on Sunday. He detached Corporal Rhazis and fifteen men for the task. But since his area of patrol reached only as far as Pikermi, he also dispatched a mounted gendarme to his colleague, Lieutenant Angelos Georgiou, at Kato Souli near Marathon, ordering him to patrol the eastern section of the route, between Pikermi and Marathon. This mounted soldier, sent off shortly after midnight on Monday morning, did not reach Kato Souli until Monday midday, by which time the excursionists had already reached their objective in safety. Why it should have taken him nearly twelve hours to cover the few miles along a carriage road is a point which seems very material, but which was never explained or even enquired into.

Monday dawned. At five-thirty the carriages drew up outside the hotel. Vyner, whose propensity for sleep had won him the nickname of Dormouse, was somehow got out of his bed. And shortly before six o'clock a start was made. In the leading carriage rode Herbert, the Muncasters and Vyner, with Sayandas and Alexander on the box. In the second were Lloyd, his wife Julia, his daughter Barbara, a little girl of six, and Count de Boÿl, with the spare coachman and de Boÿl's Italian valet, Domenico Roella, up in front. Muncaster had wished to find a place for his Swiss courier Lewis Gleissner; but the inclusion of Roella prevented this, and Gleissner, luckily for himself, stayed behind. The day was fine. None of the travellers, despite some jesting talk on the previous evening, had the smallest apprehension of danger, as the presence of the women and child makes very clear. They clattered along the Kephissia boulevard. At Ambelokipos they were met by their four mounted gendarmes, who attached themselves two in front of and two behind the cavalcade. And they trotted off happily eastwards into the Attic countryside and into the sun, which rose clear and warm above Mount Hymettus.

That evening at seven o'clock, Mr. Thomas Cook entered the salle-à-manger of the Hotel d'Angleterre with some English tourists whom he was conducting to the sites of classical antiquity. Three chairs were tilted forward in token of reservation. Mr. Cook asked Polyzoïs who the expected strangers were. They were English lords, was the reply, who had gone with friends on a trip to Marathon. They had been discussing the expedition at dinner last night, and had laughed and joked over the possibility of their capture by brigands. Mr. Cook ate his dinner; but when he had finished it, the reserved seats were still unclaimed.

The carriage party had made good progress, and had reached Marathon by eleven-thirty. The scene was familiar to many, and Lord Byron's description of it to all: of the narrow strip of coastal plain stretching between the pine-clad spurs of Pentelicus and the blue waters of the Euboic Channel; the frowning peaks of Euboea beyond the strait; the reedy marshes to north and south; and, in the centre of the southern half of the plain, the red Mound, thirty feet in height, which covered the dust, as yet undesecrated, of the one hundred and ninety heroes who had died for Greece and Europe so long ago. The party stopped, and lunched. They viewed the Mound, and walked the half mile down to the sea. Then, as it was two o'clock, it was time to begin the long drive home. Muncaster asked Alexander if they could not return by a different road; but Alexander vetoed this proposal. The carriages were filled as before, and were about to drive off. But at this moment a body of twelve foot-soldiers was seen to be approaching from the direction of Kato Souli, where Lieutenant Georgiou had at last got his men on the move. The detachment was led by two corporals, Dimitropoulos and Kandas, and by a guide, Spyro Kamboutzis, whose authority was superior to theirs. And now occurred one of the most crucial and confusing incidents of the whole affair. According to the plain and repeated testimony of Kamboutzis, supported by his corporals, he made it clear at once to the mounted escort and to Alexander that the detachment had been sent out from Kato Souli to guard the travellers, and that the latter must therefore drive slowly in order that the foot-soldiers might keep them in sight. On learning of their mission, Lloyd had offered them a twenty-five drachma note as a *pourboire,* which, after an explanation by Alexander, was accepted by them. This account was confirmed by the testimony of Roella. The party then proceeded quietly for half an hour to a well where the horses were to be watered. While this lengthy operation was in process, Kamboutzis and his men again came up with them, and the warning about not going too fast was reiterated to Alexander. When the watering was finished, the carriages drove on; but in a different order, for either Alexander or Sayandas said: 'let him [that is, the other coachman] go first, as he knows the way better.' So the Lloyds' carriage took the lead. This was another interesting circumstance which was never properly sifted there could be no question of one coachman's knowing the single road better than the other, and the suspicion is unavoidable that either Alexander or Sayandas, or both, had reasons for wishing to be behind rather than in front.

The carriages soon overtook the soldiers of Kamboutzis, who were only a short way ahead, at the stone bridge of Xylokeriza. For the third time Kamboutzis shouted his warning. But the coachmen took no heed; and one of the mounted gendarmes said laughingly to Kamboutzis, 'As they will not stop, are you then eagles to keep pace on two legs with us who go upon four?' The cavalcade drove on at a round pace, and was soon out of sight.[1]

Now, all this damning evidence was utterly denied by Alexander. He denied, that is to say, that any such warning had ever been given, let alone three times, by Kamboutzis. All he would admit was, that at the halt by the well he had asked Kamboutzis if he had any messages for Athens, and that Kamboutzis had given his regards to a friend or two there. In this denial Alexander was supported by the two mounted gendarmes who were afterwards able to give evidence. The coachman Sayandas, Alexander's hireling, prudently stated that he had heard nothing at all, being, at least on the second occasion, busy drawing water. Of the other available witnesses, the Muncasters, Julia Lloyd and Roella, the first three knew no Greek and the fourth almost none. Muncaster deposed[2] that at the first appearance of the detachment Alexander had said, 'Those men

---

[1] Roella's testimony: Sir A. Paget to Clarendon, 25 May 1870.
[2] Muncaster to Clarendon, 10 May 1870.

have nothing to do with you: they are on police duty and are returning to Athens'; and that, when Lloyd enquired whether the twenty-five drachmas given to the soldiers was enough, Alexander seemed put out, and repeated that the soldiers had no connexion whatever with the excursion. There was thus on this vital matter an absolute conflict of evidence. Either Kamboutzis or Alexander was lying. We need not at this stage decide between them, since other evidence bearing on the question was later to come to light.

The journey homeward proceeded uneventfully for about two hours. Shortly after four o'clock the carriages met the detachment of fifteen foot-soldiers sent out from Kephissia under Corporal Rhazis. This detachment also they passed; and it turned about to follow them. At about four-fifteen the party, now some hundreds of yards ahead of Rhazis' soldiers, were approaching Pikermi, where the horses would be changed. Half a mile short of this place the road bent to the right and began a gentle descent towards the bridge which spanned the wide ravine of the Megalo Revma: a torrent which, rising in the heart of the Pentelicus, poured down to discharge its waters into the sea at Raphina. The spot is now in fairly open country; but at that time both sides of the road were thickly overgrown with pine and shrub, and the plane trees, already in leaf, which grew in the ravine itself gave impenetrable cover to its precipitous banks.

The cavalcade approached the bridge at a rapid trot. There was a sudden loud cry of 'Ston dópo.'[1] In a second the road was swarming with twenty armed ruffians. The two leading gendarmes swung themselves from their saddles. But, before they could reach their carbines, a volley of musketry laid them both, with one of their horses, in the dust. Their comrades in the rear were quickly overpowered. The travellers were ejected from their seats in a twinkling, Constance Muncaster's descent being hastened by a blow from a stick. They were forced up the bank

[1] 'Halt!'

on the north side of the road, and urged forward at the top of their speed over the rolling country towards the mountain. Alexander, who, not for the last time, attempted to slip away in the confusion, was sighted and collared, amid cries of 'dragománo mazí' ('the dragoman too'). The carriages, the coachmen, the two wounded gendarmes and the dead horse were left in possession of the field.

Sayandas and his colleague put the two wounded men into a carriage. One of them was hit in the jaw, the other mortally wounded by a shot in the stomach. This carriage Sayandas drove off at once to Athens. The other carriage trotted away to the nearby village of Harvati, and there it waited for the ladies: the coachman knew, he said, that brigands always released women as soon as they could, and he would take them back to Athens. All in all, it was as pretty an *enlèvement* as could have been devised.

The incident however had occupied some minutes. The retreat was hardly under way before the detachment of Corporal Rhazis, which, on hearing the first shot, had begun to run towards it, arrived at the scene of the encounter. The fugitives were still quite close, and in full sight. The soldiers opened a brisk fire in their general direction, and the brigands returned it. The prisoners were forced to the ground for their own safety, as the balls whistled round them. The brigand chief told Alexander to stop the firing, and this he contrived to do by waving a white handkerchief. The soldiers understood his meaning only too well, and allowed the party to withdraw unmolested. In the fusillade only one brigand had been hit, and he only slightly. The soldiers were untouched. Yet the distance between the parties was not much more than fifty paces.

The light was beginning to fail; and the brigands were concerned to make good their retreat to a place of safety before darkness fell. Lady Muncaster and Mrs. Lloyd were put on two of the surviving horses, and Lloyd, with Barbara in his arms, followed on the third. The rest were hastened forward as fast as their legs would carry them. The going for the first hour was rough but not steep, and it was not until the final ascent of the low peak of Daù Pendéli, that those on foot began to feel fatigue. Their greatest danger was the poor child Barbara. She was thoroughly frightened and, though carried by her father, she cried and screamed without cessation. The chief was so much incensed at this betrayal of his position that the wretched parents were for a time in an agony lest he should decide to silence their infant in the most effectual manner.

But at length, after two-and-a-half hours' climbing, the deserted peak was gained, and captives and captors could take stock of one another. The captives were first relieved of whatever valuables they had about them. Their identity wars next elicited; and when their social and diplomatic importance was known, the brigands could not refrain from dancing in their joy. This was later urged as a proof that they had not until then known who their prisoners were, but of course it proves no such thing. It is possible to rejoice that an expected *coup* has been successfully carried out. Or again the fact, if fact it were, that the rank and file knew nothing of the prisoners till that moment is no proof that their chiefs were equally ignorant.

The brigand band was found to number twenty-one. Its leaders were two brothers, Dimitrios, or 'Takos', and Christos Arvanitákis. They, with their cousin Stathakis and another crony named Patsiouras, formed a governing council, which kept its plans to itself and exercised an iron discipline over the subaltern crew. The chief, Takos, had been longest in the business, and his career was typical of many. He was one of the seven sons of a Vlach or shepherd family of Agrapha. As his Vlach descent was later insisted upon to show him a foreigner, it must be said that the term was then very loosely applied to any nomadic shepherd: and in fact the word 'Vlachos' was synonymous with the other names of a shepherd, 'tsobánis' and 'poimín'. Takos and his family were in all probability not Wallachians, still less Albanians, but of the race of nomadic herdsmen more properly termed 'Sarakatsans'; and modern scholarship is agreed that the Sarakatsans are of pure Hellenic stock, although the riddle of their name has not so far been satisfactorily solved.[1] Takos had taken part in the Greek invasion of the Turkish provinces in 1854. The invaders were expelled, but managed to carry off with them 10,000 head of cattle and 40,000 sheep, looted from their Christian brethren, and Takos and his brother Dinos set up for drovers. The former, however, finding that it was easier to raise money by pillage and extortion than by dealing in cattle, took to brigandage, and by 1860 had advanced to the front rank in his profession. For a short time he deserted the mountains, and, through the influence of his patrons in Athens, secured the post of a guide in the militia; but he soon obtained a discharge and returned to a life of robbery. By 1867 he had amassed considerable wealth. In this year, as we have seen, Mr. Koumoundouros, the prime minister, had summoned the country's brigands to a parley at Phournes, not far from Karpenisi; and among them Takos, tricked out in silver ornaments and leading a pet ram with a chain of gold medallions slung from horn to horn, cut no inconsiderable figure. He elected to participate in the diversionary expedition into Thessaly which was then being organised by the Koumoundouros government, and was slightly wounded in that enterprise; though, as he told Herbert, he did not take credit for much patriotism. Thereafter, it was the mountains again, and abduction, and pillage, and murder, together with such secret political assignments as were given him by his protectors. His brother Christos had joined him a few years earlier; after suffering an examination under torture by the militia, to induce him to give information as to Takos' whereabouts.[2]

[1] Höeg, I, 74– 94; see Consul Stuart to Clarendon, 9 June 1870.
[2] Finlay, *The Times*, 3 June 1870; Noel, *Letters*, 52.

The rest of his crew, all but three of them, had been born across the frontier, and were thus, technically speaking, Turkish nationals. These were however all Greek-speaking, and all Orthodox Christians: the very men indeed whose liberation from the Turkish yoke was the justification urged for every Greek act of aggression in Thessaly and Epiros; and the very men whom Greece had employed to carry out those acts. For these reasons the Greek government of 1870 found some difficulty in disclaiming all responsibility for them and in dismissing them as a gang of alien malefactors. The plea seemed not to carry conviction.

Such was the band of wild and dirty wretches who, at seven o'clock on 11 April, at the top of Daù Pendéli, surrounded Lord Muncaster and his party, and began, through the mediation of Alexander Anemoyiannis, to discuss terms for the party's release. The intial conference was short. Takos was so much elated by the importance of his prisoners that he there and then fixed a ransom of a million drachmas, or 32,000 English sovereigns. The prisoners demurred; but the sum was written down, together with the usual demand for a cessation of all pursuit, in a letter addressed to the minister of war, General Soutzos. Herbert scribbled a note to the same effect for Mr. Erskine. These missives were entrusted to the two gendarmes and to Constance Muncaster respectively. The gendarmes were ordered to proceed at once to Athens with the women and child, and with de Boÿl's servant Roella. At parting Takos suggested to Lady Muncaster that she should send him a gold chain from Athens as a memento of their brief acquaintance, a request which she could in the circumstances hardly refuse; but in return she asked for, and received, the silver medallion of the Virgin that he wore round his neck. She and Julia Lloyd were then set on two of the horses, and the long descent to the high road began. The night was dark, and the gendarme guides repeatedly lost the track. It was not until after nine o'clock that they reached the carriage waiting for them at Harvati; and not until after eleven that, with Barbara at last mercifully asleep, they drove up to the door of the English Legation.

Their news had of course preceded them by some hours, when the two wounded gendarmes had been driven into Athens by Sayandas at about half-past six. The faithful courier Gleissner looked for his patrons' return; and about seven o'clock began to feel uneasy. A little later, news was brought to him by a fellow courier that 'people were saying' his employers were in the hands of brigands. He put on his hat and ran the few paces to the Legation. He told Mr. Erskine of the rumour that was afloat. At first Erskine pooh-poohed the story. 'My dear man,' he said, 'I don't believe it, nor would you, if you knew Greece. They are all liars.' But Gleissner insisted, and at last prevailed on Erskine to go with him to the house of General Soutzos. Yes, said Soutzos, it was all too true. He had already taken steps to alert the military and discover the gang. Erskine returned in deep anxiety to his Legation. The arrival of Lady Muncaster and Mrs. Lloyd two hours later confirmed what he already knew. He read Herbert's note: 'Do what you can to stop the troops from pursuing us. The captain says he requires 32,000 *l.* Our "friends" say they can be heard of in town, and request that a proper person may be sent to treat with them. Please telegraph to Carnarvon.' Erskine at once repaired, for the second time, to General Soutzos, and begged for an assurance that all military activity should cease forthwith: and this assurance was given.

Edward Morris Erskine was fifty-three years old. His career in the diplomatic service had been steady rather than brilliant. He had been six years English minister at Athens; yet he knew scarcely anything of Greece or Greeks, and what he did know he disliked. He was altogether unfit to cope with the crisis that was now coming upon him. He was, during several weeks, to stand in the searching light of world publicity, and to see his every act, almost his every thought, scrutinized, debated and finally condemned. His whole career was to be ruined, and his troubles were at last to drive him out of his mind. Mercifully, all this was concealed from him as, somewhat comforted by General Soutzos' assurance, he made his way home through the beating rain to bed.

# CHAPTER THREE

# THE NEGOTIATIONS

Shylock, the world thinks, and I think so too,
That thou but lead'st this fashion of thy malice
To the last hour of act; and then 'tis thought
Thou'lt show thy mercy and remorse more strange
Than is thy strange apparent cruelty.

THE MERCHANT OF VENICE

In the spring of 1870 the Greek government was presided over by Mr. Thrasyvoulos Zaïmis, who had been brought to power in February 1869 with the chief task of settling the Turco-Greek quarrel over Crete. The gallant but indecisive resistance to Turkey of the islanders, supported by the intrigues of Russia, had come to an end when Russian support was withdrawn. In January 1869 a treaty was composed at Paris which confirmed Turkish possession of Crete and called upon Greece to disarm. Neither of the two chief party-leaders in Greece, Mr. Bulgaris and Mr. Koumoundouros, was prepared to compromise his position by signing it. Mr. Zaïmis agreed to do so. But his government, though it had the support of a majority in the House of Representatives, was an unusually weak one; and, according to custom, the heads of the opposition parties had instantly combined against it, and thought of little else but to devise or exploit an occasion for driving it from power. The government had received some accession of strength when, in January 1870, King George had persuaded the most trusted of his advisers, Mr. Spyridon Valaoritis, to become foreign minister. Valaoritis had made it a condition of his acceptance that the war minister, General Soutzos, who was especially odious to him, should resign. He was induced by Zaïmis to waive this demand, at least for the time; but, as it turned out, he would have been wiser to insist upon it.

In the early days of April, as luck would have it, both the king and the prime minister were absent from Athens on a tour of the Cyclades. And when the capture of Lord Muncaster's party became known, Erskine was during the next forty-eight hours left to deal alternately with Mr. Valaoritis and General Soutzos.

However, at first there was no cause for alarm: or at least no alarm was felt, either in Athens or London. On Tuesday morning, 12 April, Soutzos came to Erskine and confirmed to him that, in view of the brigands' demand for the suspension of pursuit, all orders to the military had been countermanded. The next task was to fix on an emissary who should seek out the brigands, and open negotiations with them. Soutzos had a suggestion to make. He was thoroughly familiar with the circumstances of the Arvanitákis family, and thus knew that one of Takos' brothers was a cattle-dealer named Dinos. This Dinos and three of his non-brigand brothers had stood in some sort of relation, not at that time precisely understood, to a Mr. Francis Noel, the English proprietor of an estate in the island of Euboea and a friend of Edward Herbert. This connexion suggested to Soutzos that Dinos Arvanitákis might be a suitable go-between, and he proposed to Erskine that a message should be sent to Noel asking him to send Dinos out in search of his brigand brothers. Erskine wrote a telegram to Noel in this sense, and entrusted it to Soutzos. The General also stated that he had received a more recent communication from Takos which increased the ransom demanded from £32,000 to the preposterous sum of £50,000. This should, and no doubt could, be reduced.

On returning to his office, Soutzos discovered that the services of Dinos Arvanitákis were not available, since he had left Athens for Salonika shortly before, to buy cattle. He therefore suppressed Erskine's telegram to Noel, without informing Erskine of the fact, and determined on another envoy.

Dwelling in a cottage in the hamlet of Xylokeriza, near Marathon and on Soutzos' own estate, was a Vlach, or shepherd, named Costa Seliamis. He was well known to the police as a bad character, a thief of cattle and honey, and an agent of brigands, who used him as a bearer of their mandates to the peasantry. The brigands, for their part, regarded him, with good reason, as a government spy. His brother was at that moment in the Mendresé prison at Athens, serving a long sentence for robbery.

Now, this Seliamis had been on the spot at the time of the abduction; and the close relationship in which he stood to the Arvanitákis gang was clear from the fact that it had been he who had come to General Soutzos' house late on Monday night with the brigands' demand for a ransom increased to £50,000. This person was now fixed on by the minister of war, who consulted neither his ministerial colleagues nor Mr. Erskine, to be his envoy with at least a semi-official status. The officer commanding the flying-column in Attica, Captain Moschovakis, was ordered to bring Seliamis to Athens without delay, and by Tuesday evening Seliamis and Soutzos were again in conference. According to the later testimony of Moschovakis, Seliamis was told that his mission was simply exploratory: he was to find out where the brigands were and to open the way to official negotiations. He was then put in a carriage and, accompanied by a mounted sergeant, was driven back to his village of Xylokeriza. Thence a short while after he set off, with no uncertain tread, into the mountain.

Meanwhile, on the Monday night, Takos and his band, after dismissing the female prisoners, had hastened to put as much distance as possible between themselves and the scene of their exploit. The weather, which from now on played an important part in the proceedings, had turned very foul. It rained and blew hard. All night the brigands pushed on over the mountain, with one brief pause for refreshment at two in the morning. They skirted the Mavrinora and the eastern slopes of the Pentelicus, crossed the head of the valley of Rapendosa, and at last, as dawn came, established their *liméri* in a copse on the northern foot-hills, a little way above the village of Stamata. The rain stopped, and the sun came out fitfully. Once a file of sixteen soldiers was seen passing along the road below; but, to the relief of the brigands, and to the greater relief of the prisoners, no alarm was given, and quiet again prevailed.

The day passed in serious bargaining. The ransom demanded then stood at £50,000. But at some point during Tuesday's negotiations it was suggested that this demand should be changed to *either* a ransom of £25,000 *or else* an amnesty or free pardon. That this modification was finally agreed to by all parties on Tuesday, 12 April, admits of no doubt, since these were the terms brought back to Athens by Muncaster on 13 April. The point is important as proving that the idea of though not the insistence on, an amnesty must have originated either with Takos and Christos or else with the captives. It cannot have been suggested by Soutzos through Seliamis, since Seliamis did not discover the band until the following day. Nor can it have been suggested to Takos by any authority in Athens before the abduction: since, had that been so, Takos would not initially have demanded sums of money without mentioning an amnesty at all. The point was rightly seized on by Greek apologists, who claimed that Muncaster himself had put the idea of an amnesty into the heads of his captors: and evidence to this effect was later given by the brigand Karavidas. What seems more probable is that the brigand chiefs, who were exceedingly well off already and who throughout the subsequent negotiations made no secret of their desire for a 'return to the world', put forward the idea, and that the captives eagerly snatched at it as a means of saving their own pockets, without any knowledge of the constitutional difficulties which such a demand would encounter. For, by the thirty-ninth article of the new Constitution of 1864, a free pardon without trial was expressly forbidden in criminal cases.

At all events the bargain was struck, and it was necessary to have its terms conveyed to Athens by a responsible personage. Takos agreed that one of his captives should go, and left it to them to choose him. Humanity suggested that one of the two married men, Muncaster or Lloyd, should be selected. But there was also the question of which of the two was in the better position to raise the sum of £25,000 in the shortest time. Lloyd was a poor man, heavily in debt. Muncaster was indeed not very well to do; but his brother-in-law, Edgar Drummond, was a rich merchant banker, able and doubtless willing to make the sum available in two or three days' time. Muncaster, with genuine reluctance, agreed to go. He was a brave and honourable man, and the base imputations afterwards made against his courage and honour by John Gennadios neither merited nor received attention. He gave Takos his word as a gentleman that he would obtain either the money or the amnesty: failing which he would return to captivity.

The day was now far spent. Muncaster could not find his way back to Athens, and nobody could at that hour be found to conduct him. As soon as darkness fell, the whole company was once more on the move. The rain was falling again, and the prisoners, who were without the impenetrable felt capotes worn by all the countrymen of those parts, were soon drenched and shivering. They descended westwards from their hill into the plain which separates the Pentelicus from Mount Parnes, and in a few hours they were near the road that leads northwards from Kephissia. In a pine wood they lay down to repose, but in such acute discomfort not even the somnolent Vyner could sleep. He was indeed so thoroughly chilled that he could put up with the nauseous proximity of a brigand, who kindly lay close to him and imparted some animal warmth. At dawn the party moved, still with the utmost caution, a few miles further towards the west, and there they lay up beneath the shelter of pines near Keramidi, for the day which continued overcast, and in the rain which continued to pour down over them.

At nine o'clock on Wednesday morning brigand scouts brought in two local woodcutters, one of whom, Lazaros by name, was the proprietor of a horse and cart. He was bidden to drive Muncaster forthwith into Athens, an order which, needless to say, he very promptly obeyed. At half-past noon this singular conveyance drew up at the Hotel d'Angleterre. Muncaster, jaded and soaked to the skin, got down and entered; and Erskine soon joined him. Now for the first time authentic information was to be had of the prisoners' condition. It was a cruel stroke of fortune which had turned the usually warm and serene weather of April into cold and rain more suitable to January; and Erskine was apprehensive of the effect, especially on the delicate constitution of Herbert, of being dragged night after night through wet pine-woods and resting by day in soaking clothes. The ransom was the least of the difficulties. As had been anticipated, Edgar Drummond at once agreed to put up the whole, as did Lord Carnarvon, who had hurried to London from Ventnor on receipt of the news of his cousin's abduction. But, on that very Wednesday, long before an answer could be got from either, the sum was made available, on the bare word of Muncaster and Erskine, by Mr. Merlin of the Ionian Bank. Erskine knew, better than the captives, something of the difficulties that the alternative demand for an amnesty would create. He was therefore the more astonished, on meeting General Soutzos that morning, to learn that Soutzos was in favour of granting this; and his amazement grew as the General blandly added, 'the brigands are no worse than other men who are considered honest': a sentiment which, however true, came oddly from the mouth of the minister of the Crown whose duty it was to extirpate them.[1]

[1] Erskine to Clarendon, 25 May 1870.

While negotiations were proceeding to get together the ready money, measures were taken to relieve the hardships of the prisoners. Polly was active in procuring warm clothing; and this, with ample supply of provisions, was sent off in the cart of Lazaros. With Lazaros went Domenico Roella, to minister to de Boÿl and to carry a note from Muncaster to Vyner with the news that the ransom was assured. Their departure was witnessed by a large crowd who had already got wind of Muncaster's arrival. And much indignation was felt at seeing, instead of a strong force of troops, a cartful of supplies dispatched to the lair of the miscreants. This sentiment the opposition newspapers of course did their best to inflame.

Meanwhile at Keramidi events were assuming a more serious posture. Soutzos' agent Seliamis, after tracking his quarry over the mountain during all Tuesday night, came on their traces at Stamata on Wednesday morning, and on Wednesday evening established contact with themselves, in a peasant's hut where they had taken shelter after dark. What passed between Takos and Seliamis at this the first meeting between the government's agent and the gang was never accurately known. But the result of the conference was a third revision of Takos' terms: he now said that he would have both the ransom of £25,000 and the amnesty for his band, and he told Seliamis to carry these demands back to General Soutzos. In view of the General's own expression to Mr. Erskine a few hours earlier, we shall not be far wrong in supposing that Seliamis had derived from Soutzos himself the impression that an amnesty would probably be granted; and that, in view of this, Takos saw no reason to make a sacrifice of £25,000 for something which could as easily be got without it. Four quite distinct sets of terms had now been formulated by Takos in the short space of forty-eight hours. Where was this to end?

Thursday, 14 April, was of decisive importance. It was taken up with to-ing and fro-ing between Athens and Keramidi, where the brigands still lay. Four separate parties were engaged in negotiating with Takos: the English and Italian ministers, the Greek government, General Soutzos on his own account, and another party whose identity was mysterious. At noon the king and queen and the prime minister returned to Athens from Syra. The king at once received Mr. Erskine. His Majesty was nearly prostrated by the occurrence, expressed his liveliest regret, and was indeed so much moved as to make the frantic proposal that he should put himself into the hands of Takos as a surety for the prisoners' safety. He confirmed in his own name and in that of Zaïmis the promise of Soutzos that no military action should be undertaken against the gang while the captives remained in their hands. And he added that whatever moneys were needed for ransom should be found by his government. In much of this he was exceeding his own powers, as he subsequently discovered; but grief and shame made him incautious in what he said.

Meantime a council of ministers had hastily been summoned, and the latest demands of Takos were before it. The demand for an amnesty, now no longer alternative but additional to the ransom, was manifestly in direct contradiction to that article of the Constitution which stated that the king's pardon without trial could be granted only in civil, and not in criminal, cases. Soutzos, when he told Erskine the day before that an amnesty could and should be given, had clearly been ignorant of this provision, which had been written into the code for the very purpose of stopping the indiscriminate use of the royal prerogative, so often exercised by King Otho, in pardoning notorious bandits and outlaws. Mr. Zaïmis and his collegues saw very clearly to what such a constitutional violation, if they were to allow it, would lead: namely, to their own defeat and expulsion from office; and they made it plain to General Soutzos, and to Mr. Erskine, that an amnesty was impossible. It was bad enough to have to acquiesce in the suspension of pursuit of the criminals: to be blackmailed into pardoning them illegally they altogether refused. In view of the fact that nearly everybody in England from Lord Clarendon downwards, and a sizeable part of the population of Greece herself, thought that the Greek government should have given way on this point, it ought to be stated as emphatically as possible that Zaïmis and his cabinet were absolutely right in their decision, and were only doing what any responsible body of representatives must have done.

Their decision was at once communicated to Erskine and to his Italian colleague, Count Della Minerva. On the same day Roella had returned from Keramidi, bringing a letter addressed by Takos to Erskine and Della Minerva personally. Vilely written by the brigands' clerk Zomas, at Takos' dictation, this letter ran as follows: 'Mr. minister of england and of italy, gents are very well but what we agreed with the gent [i.e. Lord Muncaster] about the ransom 25 thousand pounds we also demand of the greek government the amnesty and the pursuits are to be stopped because when we see pursuit the gentlemen are in danger and not only in attica but in all the provinces and we expect your answer tomorrow without fail.' This communication was accompanied by a note from Herbert, saying, 'they want an answer in Greek to their letter.' What was Mr. Erskine to do?

It was here that he made the first of his major blunders. He decided to answer Takos' letter there and then, in his own name. It does not seem to have occurred to him that in doing so he was assuming a responsibility to which he had no title at all, and which he would be quite unable to shoulder. By putting himself into direct communication with Takos, he was pledging his own honour and that of his country to an observance of the contents of his letter; and he should first have asked himself whether his country was in any position to contract such obligations outside its own borders and, if so, whether

47

there was any possibility of such obligations being discharged. But all he saw was that his friends were in danger, and that he must do what he could to relieve them. Therefore, without informing the king or Mr. Zaïmis, without even referring to Count Della Minerva, he sat down and wrote as follows:

> The English and Italian Ministers have received your communication. There will be no difficulty as to the payment of the money, but you must not insist on an amnesty which government have not the power to grant. Persons will be sent to treat with you, and in the meantime both the King and Prime Minister have assured the English Minister that you shall not be molested. Make your prisoners as comfortable as you can. You can even put them under cover in some rural habitation without any fear.

Thus he gave the word of an English envoy that the gang should not be molested and, at least by implication, that they might go unmolested wherever they would. This he afterwards denied, but the case is surely plain: the brigands had demanded that all pursuit should cease, not only in Attica but in all the other provinces of Greece; by failing to qualify this demand, Erskine certainly allowed Takos to assume that the condition was agreed to.

This letter Erskine was handing for translation to his interpreter Lambros, when Mr. Spiliotakis, the foreign under-secretary, entered the room. Erskine at once asked Spiliotakis to write the Greek version. Spiliotakis complied, and his version was checked with the original by both himself and Lambros. Erskine signed his name in Greek characters below. And the letter was dispatched by the government agents who were on the point of departure to Keramidi.

In the afternoon the government's embassy set out. The emissaries chosen by Mr. Zaïmis were three ministerial hangers-on, whose names were Hormovas, Ioannou and Zikos. Why they were chosen is unknown. They were certainly men of no account and little repute: one of them, Ioannou, who was entrusted by Takos with £30 to buy the weapons of the defunct General Hadji-Petros, quietly appropriated the cash, and never appeared again. To them was joined Costa Seliamis, who represented General Soutzos, and had the difficult task of persuading the brigands that the General now agreed with his colleagues as to the impossibility of an amnesty. The fifth member of the delegation was Dionysios Dragonos, Herbert's faithful valet, who brought supplies of food for the prisoners.

As darkness was falling, they approached the brigands' lair. Seliamis, who from his previous visit knew what was to be done, fixed a red handkerchief on a stick, waved it, and cried, 'Captain George Trakosari'. The party was admitted into a large hut, of which the prisoners, carefully guarded, occupied one end and the chiefs the other. Negotiations were begun at once, and continued during several hours. The prisoners were out of ear-shot, and could in any case not have followed the proceedings without the help of Alexander. We have thus only the account of the suspect Seliamis, who, disreputable as he was, did on occasion speak the truth, and here seems to have done so. He said that, as all four emissaries were now unanimous on the impossibility of an amnesty, Takos and Christos became slowly convinced that this was so. They accordingly, late that night, wrote a letter agreeing to accept £22,000 [sic] without the pardon, and entrusted this letter to Seliamis for delivery. The government delegation then took leave, and began the journey back to Athens. They had, however, not gone far when they were met by two other emissaries, who did not come from the government, proceeding in their turn to the brigands. These fresh negotiators prevailed on Seliamis to turn back and show them the way. They obtained admittance to Takos, and Seliamis sat down to wait for them. Shortly afterwards Takos came out to Seliamis. He was in high excitement and exultation. He said, 'Why have you been cheating us? These men [the prisoners] are *kings,* and we will have both amnesty and ransom! We will have whatever we like!' He then took his letter back from Seliamis and tore it up. Something like an orgy seems to have followed this exhilarating announcement. And shortly afterwards Dionysios observed with disgust Seliamis caressed and embraced by his maudlin hosts. From this time forward, the brigands were immovable. The mysterious envoys who had come second had been able to persuade them that their prize was infinitely more valuable than they had suspected. This information, together with Erskine's guarantee, made their position – as they thought – unassailable. They would impose their own terms, with the certainty that these must be granted. And their next, and final, demand was for ransom and for a general amnesty embracing every brigand, either in arms or in prison, throughout Greece!

Now, we should not be justified in accepting this account of Seliamis, even with the assurance of Captain Moschovakis, who examined him, that it appeared to be veracious, unless it were substantiated by other evidence. But it was substantiated, to the letter, by the accounts of Mr. Zaïmis, of the prisoners, and of Alexander. The chief point impressed on Takos by these anonymous envoys was that he now had, as he said more than once, 'kings' in his hands. What he meant by this he made clear to Alexander next day. 'I hear,' he said, 'that the gentleman we let go [Muncaster] was cousin of the Queen of England.' And on 16 April Vyner wrote to Muncaster, 'There is someone in the background at Athens, who fills his [Takos'] head with extravagant ideas; says you are the twelfth richest lord in England and first cousin of the Queen.' Both Alexander and Vyner tried to disabuse him of this error, but in vain: and he repeated it to Colonel Theagenis on 20 April. Whoever that 'someone in the background at Athens' might be who had sent this information to Takos, he certainly dealt a fatal blow to any prospect of a reasonable settlement.

As for the error itself, it is not very difficult to see how it arose in the mind of the mysterious informant. Muncaster was of course not connected with the Royal Family. But there was an obscure peer, William George, second Earl of *Munster*, who, as grandson of William IV by Mrs. Jordan, was in fact Victoria's first cousin at one remove. The person in Athens obviously made this false identification. It is likely that he looked into a list of the Peers of Parliament, such as he might find in a publication as well known as *Whitaker's Almanack;* where Munster, as an English earl, would be listed, and Muncaster, as an Irish baron, would not. No notice was taken of the point at the time. Yet it surely follows that whoever was familiar enough with English and English handbooks to make the identification was in a very different class from the illiterate Seliamis, on whom the Greek enquiry sought to pin responsibility for Takos' intransigence.

Seliamis' whole account of his double mission to Takos on Thursday, 14 April, first with the government envoys and then with the others, was accurately and concisely borne out by Mr. Zaïmis, who visited Erskine in great distress on the following morning.

At first [wrote Erskine to Lord Clarendon][1] the brigands seemed disposed to accept a ransom of 22,000 *L* on condition that hostages be given to ensure their reaching the frontiers in safety; but in the course of the night they were visited by persons from Athens, who are believed, by M. Zaïmi, to have been despatched by some of the leading members of the opposition, and who persuaded the brigands to insist on a unconditional amnesty not only for themselves, but for all their companions now in prison – the supposed object being to compel the Government to convoke an Extraordinary Session of the Chamber, and thus afford the opposition a fresh opportunity of defeating the Ministry and driving them from office.

[1] Erskine to Clarendon, 16 April 1870.

The dispatch in which this intelligence was conveyed to Lord Clarendon became the most notorious among all the many thousands to which the Dilessi affair gave rise, and it is perhaps the only one which is not forgotten even today. Why it should have achieved this notoriety must be explained in a later chapter, when we come to discuss – not indeed its significance, for that alas! was all too plain – but the importance attached by the Greeks to its publication. Suffice to say that a wiser man than Erskine would have marked as 'confidential' a document which contained so very frank an appraisal of the political interests involved in the abduction from the mouth of the prime minister of Greece. Yet for this blunder Erskine shared the responsibility with Mr. Zaïmis and also with the English foreign secretary, Lord Clarendon; and none of the three was very much to blame. It never occurred for an instant to Zaïmis that his naive exposure of what was going on would ever be published. It never occurred to Erskine that there could be any harm in repeating what Zaïmis had said to him, when the whole of Athens, from the king downwards, was saying precisely the same: as Alexander Vyzantios put it, 'what Mr. Erskine says he heard from Mr. Zaïmis he could equally well have heard in every circle in Athens.' As for Lord Clarendon, he was in such a rage when Erskine's dispatch was received on 27 April, that he had the whole of it printed and laid before the Houses next day, without even considering the harm it might do, not only to Mr. Zaïmis, but also to Mr. Erskine himself.

Takos was now at the summit of his pride and vainglory. He had negotiated as an independent power with Erskine and Della Minerva, and obtained the former's written guarantee, in which he placed absolute trust. He was assured beyond doubt that the Queen of England must be directly concerned with his captives. Advisers of high standing, both political and legal, in Athens had told him to demand the amnesty, and convinced him that this must sooner or later be given. He decided to withdraw northward towards Chalkis and Thebes, an area with which he was more familiar, and in which he had firm friends. On Friday morning, therefore, which for a wonder was fine and sunny, he set his prisoners on horses and, in broad daylight, without any attempt at concealment, marched off along the high road through Tatoï and up to the pass of St. Mercury, whence the wide sea-board of the Chalkis channel could be seen spread out below, and beyond it the snow-clad peaks of Euboea sparkled in the spring sunshine.

The frontier post of Attica and Boeotia was manned by the military. But the presentation of Erskine's talisman removed all threat of violence; and officers, brigands and captives ate a cordial and hearty luncheon together. The party then descended the long slope to the sea, and at nightfall occupied a shepherd *stani* or cluster of huts, close to the little roadstead of Skala tou Oropoú.

The conical huts of the encampment, though of rude construction, were weatherproof and commodious; and the prisoners began to pluck up heart a little. Vyner and de Boÿl had been the chief sufferers, the one from chill and depression of spirits, the other from a numb and almost continuous despair, alternating with attacks of clamorous hysteria. De Boÿl had from the first taken the gloomiest view of their predicament, and had told his man Roella as early as Wednesday that he knew they were doomed. He scarcely slept a wink, often talked wildly to himself; and indulged in bouts of passionate weeping. This conduct naturally put a severe strain on the spirits of the rest of the company, and moved even Takos to utter a word or two of contemptuous encouragement. The conduct of the brigands in general towards their captives was as kindly and considerate as circumstances allowed. 'We tended them', said one of them afterwards to the American Tuckerman, 'like babes'!' The prisoners were given ample portions of the coarse food available, and were allowed as much freedom of movement as was consistent with the maintenance of a close watch upon them. Herbert the brigands called 'the long-bearded one', Lloyd 'the married one', de Boÿl 'the Italian', and Vyner 'the boy'. Vyner especially endeared himself to them all. At the Huts, though he was still under the weather, he recovered spasmodically some of his gaiety. He ran races and tossed the boulder with his captors. He wrote up his diary, later to be blotted with his blood; and filled his sketch-book with endless drawings of brigands and scenery. Lloyd was a strong man, who suffered little. Herbert's conduct was beyond praise. With infinite patience and delicacy he comforted and advised his little flock. At the same time he maintained a close correspondence with Erskine, and with a loyalty proof against all temptation acquiesced in the feeble policies of his superior. His letters, lucid, humorous and with a perceptible note of resignation, are in themselves a noble monument to his memory.

Saturday came, and the negotiations recommenced. The government envoy Zikos returned, and Seliamis with him. But they had only the same story to tell: that amnesty was impossible, and that the gang must be content with ransom and a guarantee of safe-conduct beyond the frontiers. Takos, now perfectly convinced that whatever terms he put forward must be granted, refused to listen to any compromise. The most he would consent to do was to discuss the procedure by which the substance of his demands could be obtained. If amnesty was impossible, pardon was not. It was pointed out to him that a pardon, even if it were possible, must be preceded by a trial. As neither he nor any of his followers would, on any guarantee whatsoever from the Greek government, surrender himself for an hour into the hands of justice, he suggested either that they should be tried, convicted and pardoned *in absentia,* or else that a special court should be convened at Oropós, at which they should be present indeed, but neither disarmed nor under arrest. These procedures were of course not merely illegal but utterly farcical, and no administration worthy of the name could have agreed to them for a moment. Nonetheless, the government, on receipt of the suggestions, went so far as to take legal advice upon them; and Mr. Provelengios, the President of the Court of Cassation, returned an apple-pie opinion, which learnedly proved them incompatible with the processes of the law.

Takos dismissed the government envoys with contempt. He knew them to be men of no account; and his enhanced importance required envoys of more exalted status. Meanwhile, he was secure in Mr. Erskine's guarantee, and could afford to wait. So great was his trust in this document that he allowed his prisoners under guard to take a long ramble during the afternoon. He himself entertained the local priest; after which he announced his intention of attending divine service on the morrow, which was Palm Sunday, at the church of Skala tou Oropoú, and of taking the prisoners with him. Even in the world of Wonderland in which they had been living for six days, they could scarcely believe their ears at this proposition. They sat down and wrote their letters: Herbert to Erskine, Vyner to Muncaster, Lloyd to his wife, and de Boÿl to M. Della Minerva; and these letters, together with others from Takos, were handed over to Seliamis. Herbert's letter was afterwards published, and it summarises very vividly the uneasiness and uncertainty which harassed the minds of the prisoners while the negotiations were protracted from day to day. Takos, he said, was still adamant; and had intimated that unless his terms were complied with in two or three days, 'he will not release us, but will do the other thing.' Erskine had said that the king would undertake to pardon them if they were tried in Athens; but Takos had answered, that they might be tried in their absence and pardoned. 'We know', Herbert commented, 'that he has private communications with Athens, on which I presume he acts.' And then he added, 'I do not think we are very unhappy, though things aren't exactly comfortable. The Captain says he would throw away his gun at once if he could get pardoned. He is a hard man after letters come from Athens – otherwise amiable, as are all the band.'[1] So ended Saturday, 16 April.

On the following morning, Palm Sunday, the whole gang, escorting their prisoners, came down from the Huts to the Skala, and went into the House of the Lord to pray. Their muskets and yataghans were piled in the porch. Palm-branches, symbolic of the preliminary to the most cruel and barbarous murder in history, were distributed among the worshippers, and the service began. Among the congregation happened to be the Greek wife of a Manchester merchant, who knew something of young Vyner's family. She was touched by his handsome, care-worn face; and she thought of Lady Mary. When the service was over, with the courage and compassion seldom wanting to her sex, she went up to Takos, who was lounging at the church door, and implored him to release Vyner. He was no more than a child, she said; and his mother was a widow. Takos heard her out; and then he laughed good-humouredly. 'Don't worry about it, Ma'am,' he said, 'in a day or two they'll *all* be free!'

The company then adjourned for coffee to the house of a rich landowner, Mr. Paparrhigópoulos, and here they were joined by the newly elected mayor of the place, Mr. Oikonomídis. Takos spoke bitterly of the envoys hitherto employed by the Greek government, and he asked Mr. Oikonomídis to go forthwith into Athens and to explain to Mr. Zaïmis that a negotiator of suitable importance must be sent to Oropós without delay. The prisoners strongly supported this suggestion. At first the mayor was most reluctant to mix himself up in the business; but Herbert undertook to write him a note to Mr. Valaoritis explaining that Oikonomídis was performing nothing but a work of charity, and on this under-

[1] Herbert to Erskine, 16 April 1870.

standing he agreed to go. Herbert himself did not like the idea of opening what might be construed as an independent negotiation with the Greek foreign minister. But he saw no alternative and the note was written.

Meanwhile in Athens the sorely tried patience of Mr. Zaïmis was becoming exhausted. The return of his envoys from their second mission, with the report that no progress of any kind had been made, had convinced the government that sterner measures must now be adopted. Their own position was nearly untenable. Their hands were tied. They were treated by Takos with open contempt. The violent, but not unreasonable, attacks made on them by the opposition press for their supine acquiescence in such a degrading situation, had weakened their authority. Worse still, they were becoming the laughing-stock of Europe. General Soutzos had at first offered to lead a strong force of troops against the gang and to compel them by sudden action to relinquish their prey; but this offer, in view of Erskine's guarantee, they had been forced to decline. Now, however, some sort of military action seemed to be inevitable.

A plan was devised whereby, without apparently breaking the promise that the brigands should not be molested so long as their prisoners were with them, a sufficient show of force should be made in the eyes of the public to convince it, and the brigands, that the government would stand no more nonsense. It was proposed that troops should be posted in a circle, at some distance from and out of sight of Oropós, and that the gang should then be given to understand that, while the offer of the ransom and unhindered withdrawal beyond the borders still stood, this offer was final, and must be accepted then and there, at Oropós. No removal northwards could be permitted, and would, if attempted, be resisted by force. It is scarcely possible to believe that Mr. Zaïmis and his colleagues, in forming this plan with full knowledge of Takos' insensate confidence in his own unassailability, were not aware of the danger to which even a hint of force would expose the prisoners. In fact, they were perfectly aware of it. Zaïmis himself wrote a personal letter to his relative Mr. Rouphos, at Patras, in which he stated that, since the brigands refused to see reason, severer methods must now be adopted which, he feared, 'would end badly for the captives'. For reasons not now discoverable, the substance of this letter was communicated to the English consul at Patras, Mr. Ongley, who passed it on, in a private dispatch, direct to Lord Clarendon; and he added, 'admitting this statement to be quite correct, and from the source from which I have learnt it there is no reason to doubt it, Mr. Zaïmis knew he was sacrificing the lives of our countrymen when he sent out the troops.'[1]

But because the eyes of the Greek government were open to the risk, it by no means follows that they were not justified in taking it. In the opinion of most people, it was the least they could do, and should have been done even earlier than it was. The difficulty, clearly, was going to be to persuade Erskine, who had himself issued a general guarantee that the brigands should not be molested, and was in daily receipt of letters from Lloyd and Vyner emphasising the disastrous consequences of any military move whatever, to agree to it.

Monday, 18 April, the day on which the fate of the prisoners was to be decided, dawned chilly and overcast. The rain fell in torrents. The plan of action devised by the Greek government had to be put before Mr. Erskine; but in the meantime a further complication was introduced by the arrival from Oropós of the mayor, Oikonomídis, with Takos' demand for a fresh envoy of suitable standing. Zaïmis at once communicated the demand to Erskine, and a long discussion ensued between them as to whom the government should select for this delicate task. At length, after many names had been suggested and dismissed, Mr. Erskine bethought him of Lieutenant-Colonel

[1] Ongley to Clarendon, 22 May 1870; Clarendon to Erskine, 31 May 1870.

Basil Theagenis; and this suggestion was at once accepted by the prime minister.

A better choice it would, at first sight, have been hard to make. Theagenis, a retired army officer, aged 67, lived at Thebes, and had thus an accurate knowledge both of the topography and of the military establishments along the Attico-Boeotian border. He had the name of an experienced soldier; and had, in his youth, performed a daring exploit during the siege of Athens by the Turks in 1827, when he had carried barefoot through the enemy lines a message from the besieged to the Greek forces lying near Piraeus. He was, moreover, in high favour with the English. He had been well known to Edward Lear, and to Sir Thomas Wyse. He was a life-long and intimate friend of General Sir Richard Church, whose aide-de-camp he had been when Church had been Inspector-General of the Greek army under King Otho. And Church himself had, since 1861, been on friendly terms with the English prime minister, Mr. Gladstone. Though Theagenis knew little or no English, he had a fluent command of Italian, which would make it easy for him to communicate with at least two of the captives, Herbert and (of course) de Boÿl. That he was to fail in both the diplomatic and the military departments of his mission was what could not be foreseen. And his selection, although it was debited as yet one more blunder to the luckless Erskine, was probably the best which could have been made in the circumstances.

Theagenis, who was staying with Church in Athens, was summoned at six o'clock before the cabinet. He consented to undertake the mission, and the ministers then deliberated upon what his instructions were to be. They finally agreed as follows: Theagenis was to proceed to the brigands at Oropós. He was to expostulate with them on their withdrawal from Attica, and to tell them that the government's pledge of immunity was not intended to cover them outside it. He was then to make four

points: first, that they could take the ransom, release the prisoners, and leave Greece unhindered, by land or by sea; second,
that no amnesty could be contemplated; third, that any harm
which befell any of the prisoners would be visited on them
without mercy; and fourth, that, while the negotiations were
proceeding, they must in no circumstances leave Oropós: if
they did so, their withdrawal would be at their own risk. The
cabinet then adjourned to the English Legation, to put these
terms before the English and Italian ministers, who were to be
asked to approve them.

Mr. Zaïmis explained to Erskine what the terms implied.
Colonel Theagenis, he said, would allow a reasonable amount
of time for negotiation, and would do his best to get the brigands to accept the government's offer. If they accepted, well and
good. If not, it would be made clear to them that their position
was hopeless. There were, or would be, upwards of six hundred
soldiers in the area between themselves and the north, and no
escape would be possible. Mr. Zaïmis went on to urge that this
was now the only course which had any chance of success, in
default of granting a general amnesty, which no Greek government could countenance. There was not the slightest intention
of provoking a clash between the brigands and the military, nor
was such a clash in the smallest degree probable. If, on the other
hand, Takos and his crew were allowed to carry off their captives into mountain fastnesses in Turkey for an indefinite period, as they were threatening to do, some or all of the unfortu-
nates would succumb to exposure and privation. He added that
he had reason to believe that a firebrand named Leonidas Bulgaris was already thinking of taking the law into his own hands
if the government remained inactive; and that he might set
upon the gang spontaneously, with such local support as he
could muster. This would inevitably lead to the murder of the
captives. Would Erskine therefore agree to the government's
plan? Or would he not? Erskine thought it all over; and he lis-

tened to the pelting rain; and he remembered Herbert's lungs.
And at last he committed the most fatal and irreparable of his
blunders: 'with deep misgiving', as he afterwards said, he sanctioned the instructions given to Colonel Theagenis. His Italian
colleague followed suit.

Erskine's blunder was in great measure due to his own
defects: to his culpable ignorance of the true facts of the case,
and to his want of courage and resolution. After the publication
in 1867 of Mr. Sotiropoulos' little book, there was no excuse
for anyone, whether Greek or foreigner, to ignore the unbreak-
able law of brigands that the exercise or threat of armed force
against them must be followed by the death of their captives.
The danger was fully realised by the captives themselves, at
Oropós.[1] It was fully realised by Mr. Zaïmis and his colleagues;
and by their agent, Theagenis, who seems from the first to have
foreseen how his mission would end. It was fully realised by
Mr. Frank Noel, who afterwards wrote to his father, 'the Government giving orders to attack the brigands under any circumstances whatever, before the captives were safe, signed their
death warrant. Mr. Erskine, I feel sure, could not have felt this,
but by the Greek Government it could not have been otherwise than perfectly understood.'[2] Indeed it was realised by
everyone except Erskine. But he could not bring himself to
believe that an offer of untold wealth, with freedom to enjoy
it, could be declined by a gang of rapacious savages. Despite the
repeated warnings of Herbert, he refused to understand that
Takos and Christos were acting on advice from Athens, which
had assured them that their demands, however outrageous,
must sooner or later be met.

But, whatever might be the outcome of this final offer if
backed by force, neither the use nor the threat of force should
ever have been sanctioned by Erskine. He had certainly erred

[1] 'Lloyd to Mrs. Lloyd, 16 April 1870.
[2] Noel, *Letters*, 27.

in sending a personal guarantee to the brigand; but, having sent it, he was obliged to see to it, so far as it lay with him, that this guarantee should be honoured in every particular. If Takos had absolute faith in the advice of his Athenian patrons, he had a not less absolute faith in Erskine's pledge of immunity.[1] It seems not to have occurred to Erskine that in giving way to Mr. Zaïmis he was compromising his own and his country's honour and good faith. Takos himself had no doubt broken his word thrice in revising the terms for release; but this was no excuse for an English minister to follow his example. He might have recalled some words of Lord Macaulay: 'No oath which superstition can devise, no hostage however precious, inspires a hundredth part of the confidence which is produced by the "yea, yea" and "nay, nay" of a British envoy.' This confidence, his country's strongest asset, Erskine was now prepared to betray: not out of any lack of moral principle, but simply because he could not see what he was doing. 'Mr. Erskine', wrote George Finlay, 'has many good qualities . . . but the affair of Oropós shewed me that his judgment is weak and that he is very deficient in character. That he blundered throughout the affair was what could not be concealed, but it seemed strange to me that he blundered in a way that was unlike an Englishman. He never appeared to see where he was going.'[2]

Yet, when all is said, his position was exceedingly awkward. He could no doubt have refused to listen and washed his hands of the business: and even this negative course would have been better than the one he chose. But his only practical alternative to approving the plan of Mr. Zaïmis was to demand, in the most peremptory and threatening manner, that the amnesty should be granted: and this he felt he could not do without

[1] 'They [the brigands] have a horror of prison – mistrusting the Greek government: but they have full trust in the English government, and put more trust in Erskine's pass than anything else': Vyner to Muncaster, 21 April 1870.
[2] Finlay to Edward Noel, 19 November 1870. (N.-B.)

express instructions from the Foreign Office. The position of English envoys had undergone considerable change during recent years: partly owing to the introduction of the electric telegraph, which, faulty as it still was, had robbed them of much of their independence and initiative; and partly to the swing of English public opinion against the Palmerstonian policy of threatening less powerful countries with coercion.[1] It is certain that Lyons or Wyse would in similar circumstances have bullied the Greek government into passivity and rescued the prisoners on any terms, including an amnesty, that the brigands cared to propose: and this in the full knowledge that Palmerston or Lord John would approve their action. Takos and his political advisers had no doubt that this could and would be Erskine's course also: and their opinion was shared by that large part of the European public which had not realised that times were changed. Yet changed they were. Constitutional principles, which a grant of amnesty would violate, were known to be the peculiar care of the prime minister, Mr. Gladstone. Who was Erskine that he should venture to demand the violation of what his own government, in an especial sense, was responsible for preserving? He had waited anxiously, day after day, for a definition of the English government's attitude on this vital question; but he had waited in vain. The foreign secretary, Lord Clarendon, seemed to have been stricken by the palsy. In a series of telegrams between 17 and 21 April he left Erskine 'a free hand'; 'hoped' the brigands might be amnestied; prophesied that 'strongest indignation' would be felt in England if they were not; and ordered Erskine to continue his efforts to induce' Mr. Zaïmis to give way on the point. Only on 23 April, after news of the death of two of the captives had reached London, did Lord Clarendon telegraph, '. . . you will in the strongest terms and in the name of Her Majesty's Government require that it [the amnesty] be granted'; and then it was three

[1] Rumbold, I, 110– 12.

days too late. This hesitation astonished the world. Why should Lord Clarendon thus hold his arm? The answer was that Clarendon's arm was pinioned by an arm stronger than his, the arm of Mr. Gladstone.

Such was the state of uncertainty in which Erskine was left on the evening of Monday, 18 April. Was it after all worth risking a Palmerstonian gesture, when, if he acquiesced in the plan of Mr. Zaïmis, all might very probably turn out well?

The conduct of Zaïmis and his colleagues must be viewed in an altogether different light. They formed the legal government of Greece: and their first duty was not to the foreign captives, sorry as they might be for them, but to their country. The argument repeatedly brought against them by Lord Clarendon and the English press, that their predecessors had, even since 1864, habitually violated the law in favour of brigands, whether this were true or false, had nothing to do with the matter in hand. The Greek government were bound to uphold the Constitution, and bound to keep order. They were therefore manifestly right to refuse an amnesty, and to apply, or at all events to threaten, force against disturbers of the peace. Let us suppose for a moment – a supposition far from chimerical – that American tourists had been abducted by Irish outlaws into the mountains of Connemara. What would have been the reply of the English government to a demand from Washington that all operations against the bandits should cease, that they should be given £25,000 and a passage to New York in an English ship, and that a free pardon should be granted, not to them only, but to every Irish outlaw in or out of prison besides? The question answers itself.

Personal motives, that is to say, the desire to keep themselves and their supporters in office, naturally played a part in determining the course adopted by the Greek government. Yet it would surely be unjust to magnify these motives in assessing an action which any government would have been bound to take. If the government had declared themselves so weak and incompetent as to abandon their own laws and responsibilities to save the lives of four foreigners for whose misfortune they at least were not directly responsible, their only course would have been to resign next day; and this they naturally wished to avoid. In concentrating troops at a distance from Oropós, they were not breaking the letter of their engagement to Erskine that the brigands should not be pursued or molested. Their agent had been selected, and his instructions approved, by the English minister himself. Their moral position was unassailable. Even that convinced opponent of Greek governments and Greek democracy, Alexander Vyzantios, was bound to applaud their decision in this instance: for to yield would have been to furnish a charter of immunity to brigandage throughout the realm. While the die was thus being cast in Athens, the prisoners at the Huts were receiving a visit from Muncaster's courier, Lewis Gleissner. Lord Muncaster was in a state of anxiety scarcely less painful than that of the prisoners themselves. The tall, blond Englishman became a familiar sight to the Athenians, who eyed him with pity as he walked their streets, with bowed head and furrowed countenance, between the Hotel d'Angleterre and the English Legation. His letters from Vyner, who was his peculiar responsibility, were full of Vyner's own suggestions for ending the imbroglio; and these suggestions he passed on to Erskine, with earnest recommendations for action. Erskine had quite enough on his hands without these additional distractions: he wrote to Herbert, 'Try to prevent Boÿl and Vyner from writing anything different from what you do- what the latter says is gospel to the Muncasters, but he knows nothing of the country, is young, and cannot speak a word of the language.'[1]

On Saturday, Muncaster asked Gleissner to go to the Huts with some clean clothes and provisions, and to bring back word

[1] Erskine to Herbert, 17 April 1870.

of Vyner's condition. Gleissner readily agreed to go and, seeing his master's anxiety, offered to surrender his own person to Takos in exchange for Vyner's freedom. Muncaster doubted if the substitution would be allowed; but he agreed that the offer should be made, and, with many expressions of gratitude, dispatched Gleissner on Sunday morning.

Gleissner rode all day, and after a journey of sixteen hours reached the encampment at eleven o'clock at night. He shook hands not very cordially with Takos, who escorted him into the hut where, guarded by relays of armed ruffians, the four prisoners, with Anemoyiannis, lay by the fire asleep. 'Those gentlemen' (as he habitually termed them in his long account of the visit) woke and welcomed him with enthusiasm. They fell on the letters which he had brought them, and read them by the light of a single flickering candle. Takos, who was as eager as they to hear the news from Athens, flew into a rage on learning that still no settlement was in sight. He beat the floor with his fist, told Alexander to tell the prisoners that his terms must be met without delay, and ended with his usual threat to slit the throats of every one of them. Alexander interpreted the demand, but omitted the threat. Mr. Herbert, whose Greek carried him that far, taxed Alexander with the omission; and this led to an interesting comment from the prisoners on Alexander's general conduct. They did not say, Gleissner recorded, that they accused Alexander of being in league with Takos; but they certainly did not believe his interpreting was either accurate or complete: and he seemed to be on terms of close familiarity with members of the gang.

Gleissner retired to rest in another hut, which he had the honour of sharing with Christos Arvanitákis. He had to sleep with that worthy's legs thrust between his own, so that he was unable to stir without rousing his companion. Next morning, he took young Vyner aside, and broached the question of Vyner's release against his own surrender to captivity. Vyner would not hear of it. He, like Muncaster, was very doubtful whether this offer, if it were made, would be accepted by Takos. But he absolutely refused to allow Gleissner to make it. Gleissner, much moved, had to content himself with brushing Vyner's clothes, with examining Takos' pistols, extracted by Vyner from the chief's cummerbund, and with urging the young fellow to write to his mother, Lady Mary. Then, sore at heart, he took his leave of 'those gentlemen', whom in this life he was never to see again.

On Tuesday morning, 19 April, he was still on his way back to Athens when he fell in with Colonel Theagenis, accompanied by twenty mounted soldiers, riding towards Oropós. Despite the Colonel's assurances, he was seriously alarmed at sight of the soldiers; and this alarm was increased by his subsequently meeting with a stream of detachments, amounting by his calculation to about two hundred men, all moving in the same direction.

Erskine, mistaken as he had been in his policy, still believed in its ultimate success. He was so certain that the gang must accept the money, especially when the offer was reinforced by a threat of destruction in the event of its refusal, that he had made detailed arrangements both for handing over the gold and for securing the safe-conduct of the brigands. He proposed to send H.M.S. *Cockatrice*, a vessel prudently dispatched from Malta by Lord Clarendon on 14 April, to the Skala, with the money on board and with authority to transport the brigands to Malta, Alexandria or any other destination of their choice. He had some doubts as to how this latter authorisation would be received at home: he feared that, if time were given, Lord Clarendon might 'put a spoke in his wheel'. However, he gave the order on his own responsibility; and Clarendon, with some misgiving, sanctioned it.[1] This extraordinary proposal, though of course it was never implemented, became public property,

[1] Clarendon to Gladstone, 20 April 1870 (B.M. Add. 44134, fol. 186).

and was unmercifully derided by *The Times* of 23 April, which 'presumed that the brigands will dine at the captain's table, and part from him carrying with them his best wishes, if not his chronometer and spoons.'

Erskine had taken a further step which he believed might assist the critical negotiation of Colonel Theagenis. He had prayed the assistance of Mr. Frank Noel, who was then on his estate at Achmetaga in Euboea. As we have seen, he had sent a telegram to Mr. Noel as early as Tuesday, 12 April; but General Soutzos had seen fit to suppress it. Erskine mentioned this circumstance to the historian and Times correspondent, George Finlay, who was a close friend of the Noel family. Finlay wrote to Frank Noel to tell him of this approach, and to say that Erskine had suggested Noel's sending up one of the Arvanitákis brothers, who was in his service, to mediate with Takos and Christos. Noel received Finlay's letter on Saturday, 16 April. It was his first intimation that Erskine was to ask for his help. He saw at once that the mere dispatch to Oropós of one of the 'civilian' Arvanitákis could be of no service whatever. Nonetheless, on the following day, he left his house at Achmetaga and travelled down to Chalkis, where he put up, as he usually did, at the house of Mr. Avyerinós Averoff, whose son Michael, the deputy for Chalkis, was his intimate friend.

Noel's proceedings during the next twenty-four hours later became the subject of much controversy and misrepresentation, and several different accounts were given of them, by himself and others. It is therefore best to confine ourselves to what can positively be known of them; and that is soon told. Monday, 18 April, was market day at Chalkis. In the course of the morning Noel became aware that one of the Arvanitákis brothers, George Yannou, was in the market. At midday he sent a message summoning George to Mr. Averoff's house; and at four o'clock George came there. Noel interviewed George in the presence of Avyerinós Averoff. The conversation was limited to a statement of Noel's intention to go personally to the brigands on the following day, and a request that George, as the brother of the chiefs, should go with him: not as an agent, but as a surety. George at first demurred, but was later persuaded. He was, after all, Frank Noel's 'man', in the Greek sense of the word, and two of his brothers, Nikolaos and Apostolis, were Noel's 'spiritual kin', or 'gossips'.

George lay the night at Mr. Averoff's house. On Tuesday morning, as predicted by Finlay, a telegram came from Erskine asking Noel to send one of the Arvanitákis brothers to Oropós. At midday Noel, accompanied by his faithful steward Panayiotis Zygouris (himself an ex-brigand) and George Yannou Arvanitákis, set sail from Chalkis. And in the afternoon they landed at the haven of Skala tou Oropoú.

Noel's first act was to announce his arrival by sending up George to his brigand brothers at the village of Oropós, four miles off; whither they had moved from the Huts on the previous day. His next was to dispatch a note to Colonel Theagenis, who was arriving almost simultaneously at Markopoulon, a village some few miles south of the Skala. In this note Theagenis was asked not to proceed to the brigands before he and Noel had been able to meet and concert a plan of negotiation. The Colonel received this note late at night, and he decided to go to Oropós next day by way of the Skala, in order to bring Noel along with him.

But meantime George had reached his brother at Oropós with news of Noel's presence at the Skala. He brought with him, moreover, a letter the existence of which was unknown to Noel. This letter was unsigned, but it was of fatal import. It stated that the amnesty would certainly be granted if the brigands stood firm for it; and its authority was such as to stultify in advance anything which Theagenis might say on the other side next day. The letter was read; and then Christos set light to it and burnt it to ashes. It was decided that, though the hour was late, Christos and four of the band should go down at once to Skala, to welcome Mr. Noel and escort him up next morning. They arrived, and slept a few hours in Noel's room, and at four in the morning started out once more for Oropós. When therefore Theagenis rode into the Skala at seven, he found Noel gone, a circumstance which did nothing to sweeten the Colonel's temper, already rasped by a long ride in drenching rain. At last, however, soon after eight o'clock, the whole party, brigands, prisoners, Theagenis, Noel and George Yannou, were gathered under one roof at Oropós; and the final disastrous negotiation could begin.

CHAPTER FOUR

# GREEK TRAGEDY

'The Queen has been deeply grieved at the terrible Greek tragedy.'

QUEEN VICTORIA TO MR. GLADSTONE

26 April 1870.

Up to this point, apart from some conflict of evidence as to the relations existing between Noel and George Yannou, there is no doubt at all as to the course of events. But from the Wednesday morning until evening on the following day, almost every fact was disputed, modified or denied by the surviving parties in their own interest: and it is not easy to determine with confidence what actually took place. By Thursday night six of the most material witnesses, the prisoners and the two brigand chiefs, were either dead or missing, and could give no testimony. The account of Colonel Theagenis conflicted in many important details with that of Frank Noel; and the fact that the former at last tacitly admitted the superior accuracy of the latter, justifies us in mainly following Mr. Noel's narrative.

The brigands had removed with their prisoners from the Huts to Oropós village on Monday, 18 April. Here they had commandeered the three best houses, including that of the *paredros*, Mr. Skourtani otis. In this house Noel had found, and been warmly welcomed by, Herbert and his friends, and scarcely less warmly by Takos himself. On the arrival of Theagenis the conference began in a private room, between four persons only: Takos and Christos Arvanitákis, Colonel Theagenis and

71

Frank Noel. It was soon apparent that the chiefs were in an uncompromising humour. They scouted the notion that an amnesty was impossible. Who made the Constitution?, asked Takos. The People? Very well, then: the People must unmake it. He was equally contemptuous of the royal prerogative. 'As for Georgy,' he said, 'the politicians make him and mar him. We have kings in our hands, and what's your Georgy to them?'

No progress could be made along these lines. But when Theagenis reached the government's declaration that the brig-ands' immunity covered them only as far as the borders of Atti-ca, and that any retreat northward on their part might be opposed by the military, he met with incredulity, stupefaction and at last violent resentment. The chiefs had unshakable con-fidence that Erskine's talisman had assured them unlimited freedom of movement, and for long they could not be brought to think otherwise. Takos produced Erskine's letter and made Noel read it aloud to Theagenis, who nonetheless insisted that their movements were circumscribed. Takos retired with Noel into another room, where the latter read and explained to him the tenor of Theagenis' instructions. Takos returned in a fury. 'We will leave at once, he cried, 'and if we are attacked by the patrols, we will kill the prisoners.' Theagenis was alarmed. 'No, no,' he said, 'I don't mean that. I said you *may* fall in with patrols who will not respect the former orders of the Government.'[1]

It is to be observed that Theagenis did not directly threat-en Takos with military force, or intimate that he was already encircled: for in fact he was not. The Colonel said only that the band *might* encounter forces to the north, which *might* bar their passage. The direct orders from government to encircle and seal off Oropós were not dispatched to Theagenis until after his departure from Athens, and did not reach him until the early hours of Thursday morning. In this the government undoubt-edly blundered. If they envisaged the use of force at all, they

[1] Noel, *Letters*, 42.

should have made certain that before its use was so much as hinted at it should already be in such positions and in such strength as to make its operation immediately decisive. The Theagenis certainly saw what was coming, and before his visit to Oropós he had given orders which would concentrate troops both at Salessi and at Sykamenon. But his final order to invest Oropós was not, and could not be, given until Thursday morning. Once more hesitation and indecision were the order of the day.

But, for his impatience in the negotiations with Takos, the Colonel was afterwards very justly reprobated. The insulting carriage of Takos, and his outspoken contempt of the king and government, were too much for the Colonel's equanimity. He lost his temper − under, it is true, very trying circumstances − and he broke up the conference after about ninety minutes He later stated that he had argued with the chiefs during six or seven hours; but, when Noel insisted that the time had been little more than an hour, Theagenis reduced his own estimate from seven hours to two. The truth plainly is that the 'reasonable amount of time' promised by the government for negotiations was, by the brigands' own insolence, reduced to a matter of minutes rather than of hours or days. Theagenis had a final interview with the prisoners, in which, so completely had he lost his self command, he told them frankly that their position was hopeless, and that they must resign themselves to inevitable death; adding this only by way of consolation, that their own destruction would inevitably be followed by that of their gaolers. He then prepared to take his leave. The captives and Noel were left staring blankly into each other's faces.

What was to be done? Two essential facts stood out: first, the threat of military force had in an instant done away with the prisoners' security and their lives were now in deadly danger; second, Takos and Christos were still adamant in their insistence on all their demands. They did not care, they said, by what means the amnesty were accorded, whether by trial *in absentia* followed by reprieve, or by free pardon; but accorded it must and should be. Noel saw that the chief, if not the only, hope of saving his friends lay in getting the amnesty granted at once, if possible before the chiefs decided to move from Oropós. The Greeks afterwards tried to fasten on Noel the guilt of encouraging Takos to stand firm for the amnesty. The truth was the very reverse. Noel was in favour of an amnesty simply because Takos insisted upon it, with an obstinacy inspired, not by Noel, but by 'somebody in the background at Athens'. Noel certainly valued the lives of his compatriots above the Greek Constitution; but so, after all, did Lord Clarendon, most of Europe, and a large part of the population of Greece herself.

Noel urged the prisoners to write to Athens, exposing in the strongest terms the imminence of their danger and the absolute necessity of prompt and decisive action to relieve it. Vyner and Lloyd wrote in this sense to Muncaster. Vyner had on the previous day asked his friend to telegraph direct to Lord de Grey, 'to ask Clarendon to urge on the Greek Government to get us released, as they can do it and will, if sufficient pressure is put on them; and write to him [de Grey] or send this letter, explaining that this is no ordinary act of brigandage, but to a certain amount political.' He now wrote once more to Lord Muncaster, a letter which revealed in every line his desperation, and which, when published, inflamed to madness the excited emotions of the English, public:

> Of course, the soldiers being let loose has done away with our security, and in the first engagement with the troops we must die... Thank the King and his ministers on my behalf for their kindness, and say that I do not ask (for I am powerless to do that), but that as a dying man I implore of them humbly to grant this request of the brigands and to prevent the operations of the soldiers...The Government official [Theagenis] regards our position as beyond hope, so we must trust to God that we may die bravely as Englishmen should do. PS... No chance of a messenger; if there is, send a Bible.[1]

[1] Vyner to Muncaster, 20 April 1870.

Poor young fellow. It is hard to face death in cold blood at twenty-three. But his touching appeal served to throw into strong relief the courage and self command of Herbert, who throughout the captivity, but never more than now, showed the sterling worth of four centuries of breeding and chivalry. To Noel's remonstrances he replied only that he was a junior in the diplomatic service, and was in no position to dispute the decisions of Erskine. He added, with a delicacy worthy of his ancestor, Sir Philip Sidney, that this was doubly impossible since he was personally involved and such advice could therefore not be divorced from self interest. Instead, he wrote to Erskine: 'The Colonel tells me that the disposition of the troops is such that we cannot go northward without a collision, and he seems satisfied that, whatever the result to us of such a collision, their [the brigands'] speedy destruction would follow. I do not know that I have more to say.' All he would add on the subject of amnesty was to quote the opinion of Noel: 'Noel', he wrote, 'may, I think be of great use to us, but he seems to think all the demands of the brigands ought to be complied with.' Had he had any idea of the misrepresentation to which this postscript would be subjected, it is safe to say that he would have sacrificed his right hand rather than write the words.

Noel could not regard this delicacy as suitable to the circumstances. He took Herbert's pencil and wrote a note to Erskine in which he did not mince his words. He said that in his opinion only the most vehement measures could now avail to save the lives of the prisoners. This correspondence was entrusted to Theagenis, who quitted Oropós at midday, and made his way back to Markopoulon.[1]

Noel at once reopened his attack on Takos, and spent the rest of Wednesday in trying to get him to see reason. Although in Noel's opinion the amnesty should be given, he was by no means confident that it would be: and the whole of his advice

---

[1] Noel, *Special Memorandum*, 28.

to Takos was that the government's terms should be accepted as they stood. Takos put more trust in what was said to him by an Englishman than in anything said by a Greek; and by evening, as both Herbert and Noel observed, he was in a more conciliatory frame of mind. Noel, he said, should be his envoy. Noel should go back on the morrow to Chalkis, and thence to Athens for further talks with the Greek government. Takos and the band would stay at, or near, Oropós until Noel sent to them again. This was more encouraging. But the danger was still acute. Would it not be possible, asked the prisoners, to extend the area of free movement so as to cover Boeotia as well as Attica? Then, if the armistice were prolonged for a week or two, Herbert believed that a solution satisfactory to all parties could be reached. This partial and temporary improvement in the atmosphere was entirely due to the efforts of Noel, who seems to have done all that intelligence and tact could suggest.

Yet his painfully erected structure was a house of cards. Behind the horizon the storm was gathering which would scatter it to the winds. Clouds and rain ushered in the morning of Thursday, 21 April, whose end those gentlemen would never see. At seven o'clock Noel was ready to take his leave of them. But meanwhile the Greek gun-boat *Afróessa* had put into the Skala; and though it was in fact on a routine cruise in the Euboea channel, its arrival resuscitated all Takos' suspicions. He told Noel that he could now not consent to remain longer at Oropós. He would move to the hamlet of Sykamenon, a short distance to the north-west, across the Asopos river: and Noel must arrange that he should not be molested there. The prisoners implored him to stay at Oropós. But, with the sixth sense of a hunted animal, he sniffed mischief and determined to go. His forebodings were but too just. At four in the morning Theagenis had received at Markopoulon his revised orders from the Greek government. He was to take instant measures, with the help of troops stationed at Salessi and Skimatari, to 'seal off' and invest Oropós in such a way that escape from it northwards would be impossible. If Takos had stayed all Thursday at Oropós, this investiture would have been completed. But it could not be done in less than twelve hours. Despite his utmost expedition, Theagenis could not concentrate his forces at Salessi before midday; and it was well on in the afternoon before they came in sight of Oropós. By then the birds had flown.

Noel left Oropós in deep anxiety. At about eight-thirty he went aboard the *Afróessa*; and his anxiety became consternation when he learnt that the confidential orders for the investiture of Oropós were the common talk of the ship's officers. He at once wrote a letter to Theagenis, telling him of the intended removal to Sykamenon and of the vital importance of extending the immunity from molestation to that place. But this letter, had it been delivered – and, according to Theagenis, it never was delivered – would have come too late, for the Colonel had been many hours up and doing. The *Afróessa* steamed into Chalkis at one o'clock. Noel hastened to the telegraph office. He telegraphed to Erskine of the move to Sykamenon. 'Detachments must not pursue,' he said. 'Brigands will consent [to the government's terms].' And he sat down to wait for Erskine's answer.

Takos and his gang left Oropós at two-thirty. The prisoners were in despair; but Takos, whatever he might suspect, knew nothing positive of what was afoot beyond the hills to the west of him. He reassured the captives, promising them that their remove was temporary and that if all went well they should be back at Oropós on the following Sunday. This assurance was probably given in good faith. The brigands' movements were traditionally governed by periods of three days, which was the longest time they would willingly stay in one place. They had been three days at the Huts, and three at Oropós. They would spend the next three at Sykamenon.

The march thither would normally have taken less than an hour; but the Asopos river, owing to the recent torrential rains, was in spate, and almost an hour was spent in fording it. When Sykamenon was reached, it was nearly four o'clock. The best house was commandeered. A watch was set. Alexander Anemoyiannis was told to dress a hare for dinner. Hardly had he begun the task when the alarm was given. The troops of Colonel Theagenis, both horse and foot, had been spied advancing eastwards down both banks of the Asopos. A panic ensued. Takos drew out Erskine's talisman. He told Alexander to take it with all speed to the van of the troops, who were no more than twenty minutes off; and to demand that they should halt in their tracks. The band then divided in two. One section, under Takos, took charge of Vyner and de Boÿl. The other, under Christos, escorted Herbert and Lloyd. Then, with a protective screen of thirteen reluctant Sykamenote peasants, they streamed out of the village and up the nearest incline to the north; and set out at their best speed for Dilessi and the coast.

Alexander succeeded in finding Theagenis, and showed him Erskine's letter. Theagenis deposed that in reply he told Alexander to go back to Takos and say that if the band returned to Sykamenon, its immunity would be respected. Alexander never delivered this message: nor is it easy to see how he could have done so on foot, with the brigands running at top speed into the distance; and Theagenis made no offer to him of a horse. Some few moments were spent in transferring that part of the troops which was on the south bank of the river to the north bank; but at length the whole force was united, and began, at a quarter of an hour's distance, to follow the flying band.

Theagenis, who had thought to invest Oropós along the line of the Asopos, had withdrawn the detachments of Skimatari and Dilessi to Salessi: so that the track northwards lay open. It led over foot-hills, divided by shallow ravines and covered with scrub and brushwood. It was not difficult to traverse, and in happier circumstances made a delightful walk.[1] But the pace was killing. All the prisoners were on foot. In a little more than an hour the distance covered, over the rolling and uneven country, was seven miles. This was nothing to the hardy mountaineers. But on Herbert the strain was fearful, and in the last stages of his exodus he was pricked on like a foundering animal by the dagger-points of his escort. At a short distance from Dilessi the long ravine of Gournies drops down into a little plain, with the sea on its right hand and the 'large house' of Dilessi hamlet about four hundred yards ahead. The rearguard of the brigands was in the bottom of this ravine when the vanguard of the pursuers topped the ridge behind them. It was five o'clock. The leaders of the band with Takos were already flying in open order over the plain. The temptation to strike a decisive blow at the party still in the ravine proved too much for the excited nerves of the soldiers. It is probable that no order to attack was given by Theagenis, and that they fired spontaneously.[2] The volley took effect. Two brigands who brought up the rear fell dead. This was the signal for the butchery to begin. The two wretches who escorted the failing Herbert – their names were Yeroyiannis and Katarachias – drew their cutlasses. Herbert threw up his right arm; but two fearful cuts laid it open to the bone. Two slashes followed across his face, one of which cut through the ramus of the jaw and severed the maxillary artery. Herbert staggered ten paces from the track and fell

---

[1] Cdr. Hotham to Capt. Hillyar, 26 May 1870.

[2] Naturally, neither Theagenis nor any of his men would admit that the troops had been the first to fire; but see Erskine to Clarendon, 23 May 1870: It must be admitted that he [the Scotch engineer Yates, on board the passing *Afróessa*] and most disinterested persons who have looked closely into the matter are of opinion that the troops fired first.' The same evidence is given by Noel, Letters, 25, corroborated by the ms. note of George Finlay. Erskine's testimony is the more striking in that he was, by 23 May, necessarily a supporter of the plans of Mr. Zaïmis and the conduct of Colonel Theagenis.

on his face across a thorn-bush. As he lay, three balls from a musket were fired into his back. By a cruel chance, none of these ghastly injuries was instantly mortal; and his final moments were too horrible for description. Erskine dared not release a detailed account of them. It was not until the third time of asking by Lord Clarendon that he transmitted the clinical report of Dr. Bolton: 'He was perfectly drained of blood, the haemorrhage coming from the internal maxillary artery.' Herbert had bled to death.

So died Edward Henry Charles Herbert, of the long beard, exhausted and defaced, never again to look on the green hills of his native Somerset or the cedar-trees of Highclere. 'Poor fellow,' wrote Carnarvon to Sir W. Heathcote, 'he seemed to cling to Evelyn and me and to this place [Highclere Castle] more than anything else.' He was descended from a line which in the annals of England is associated with the noble names of Sidney and Pembroke, and with the yet nobler names of William Shakespeare and Florence Nightingale; yet in the four centuries of its nobility it could boast no gentler, more gallant heart than his. Men are in the habit of saying of such sacrifices that the victims did not 'die in vain'. Of Herbert this may be said with some approach to truth. His death did not purchase the end of brigandage in Greece. But it did mark the end of its exploitation as a political weapon. It stripped the sordid traffic of its last lingering vestiges of romance. And the world was assuredly not the loser in ringing down a final curtain on the *opera buffa* of the King of the Mountains.

At sight of this cruel deed the soldiers redoubled their fire, and five more of the brigands' rearguard, including Christos Arvanitákis, were shot down. The rest made short work of poor Lloyd, who was dispatched, with the same savagery, at a distance of some four hundred yards from the spot where Herbert had fallen.

The retreat now became a rout. Takos and those escorting Vyner and de Boÿl who had had a start of the rest, ran at full speed across the plain, through the hamlet of Dilessi and out the other side, and up the rising track which leads to Skimatari and Thebes. Quickly as they moved, it was the general opinion that they could have been cut off and surrounded on the plain: for Theagenis' force included a detachment of cavalry under Lieutenant Manousos, which on the level ground could have galloped round the flyers and assailed them from front or flank. The cavalry did no such thing. Instead, it trotted languidly forward, almost on a level with the brigands but making no attempt to arrest them. For this supposed dereliction of duty Manousos was, at Erskine's instance, afterwards court-martialled and dismissed the service. It was common gossip that he had halted to loot the body of Christos, and that he had ended the pursuit heavier by several napoleons than he had begun it.[1] But, on the evidence officially presented, his conduct may merit a more charitable interpretation: namely, that he saw that a decisive charge would be fatal to Vyner and de Boÿl as the initial volley had been fatal to Herbert and Lloyd.

Whatever the reasons, the pursuit was not pressed home. The party of Takos reached a point on the track towards Skimatari, about three miles north of Dilessi. Here the chief saw that the remains of his band must scatter for refuge. The two young prisoners were still running strongly: running, indeed, for dear life. But in the panic and the failing light they could not well be guarded. Both were pistolled from behind, and died instantly.

The night came down. On that extended battlefield the four prisoners and seven brigands lay dead. Six brigands were taken alive. Takos and the remaining seven got clear away in the groves and pinewoods that fringe the sea-board between Dilessi

[1] Erskine to Clarendon, 15 June 1870; *Blackwoods' Edinburgh Magazine,* August 1870, 253.

and Dramessi; and at eight o'clock darkness and pouring rain put an end to the pursuit. To such a lame and fatal conclusion had come the schemes of the forcible-feebles at Athens: of Mr. Zaïmis, Mr. Erskine and Lieutenant-Colonel Theagenis.

# CHAPTER FIVE

# REACTIONS

In Rama was there a voice heard, lamentation, and weeping,
and great mourning, Rachel weeping for her children, and
would not be comforted, because they are not.

MATT. 2: 18 (A.V.)

The news of the disaster burst over Europe as with the detona-
tion of some powerful explosive. To the shock of revulsion was
added the shock of complete surprise. No one had for a
moment dreamt of so bloody an issue. Nor was this strange.
Many similar abductions had recently taken place in Mediterranean countries, and their worst result had been a more or less
trifling financial loss. The sum demanded by Takos, formidable
as it was, could have been settled by Carnarvon, or de Grey, or
the Vyners, by a stroke of their pens. Men were negligent of the
perils and ruin of Mr. Sotiropoulos. They remembered the case
of Lord John Hervey, Mr. Strutt and Mr. Coore merely as a
*comedietta,* and quite forgot that while Mr. Coore was in the
hands of Captain Dellis, his life had been more than once,
owing to the proximity of the Greek militia, in extreme danger. The optimism of Mr. Erskine had been undimmed until
the last. On 16 April he wrote to Lord Clarendon: 'I do not feel
the least apprehension for their safety'; and even on 21 April,
the very day of the massacre, he 'hoped soon to be in a position to inform Your Lordship . . . that the captives have been
released.' The general feeling of security was summed up in *The
Times* leader of 16 April: '. . . there is scarcely an element of
inconvenience, and certainly none of danger, in the transaction.

. . . There is, we have said, no danger . . . ' And this complacency helps us to understand the initially languid and indecisive policy of the English Foreign Office.

The disillusionment was proportionately severe. In Greece itself the prevailing sentiments were consternation and horror. The most destructive pestilence, said the government newspaper *Aión*, could not have made a stronger impression. In a widely published poem Mr. George Paraschos described the affair as a national disaster eclipsing the sack of Psara or Chios, or the collapse of the Cretan rebellion. The very genuine grief of the Greek people as a whole was almost entirely ignored in England; yet it was striking evidence of that people's soundness of heart, in contrast to the cynicism shown by its political managers.

On none did the blow fall more crushingly than on the chief of the state, the young King George. Like everyone else in Athens he had at once recognised the affair as a political job[1], and he was nearly out of his mind with shame and dismay. *'Plaignez-moi'*, he burst out to Della Minerva, *'de devoir travailler avec des gens dont je connais la profonde immoralité. Que me sert de changer de ministre, lorsque je sais que je tombe toujours de mal en pis?'* In his resentment he vowed repeatedly that he would desert 'the country of which nothing can ever be made.'[2] On 23 April he wrote to his brother-in-law, the Prince of Wales, who was recently married to his beautiful sister Alexandra: 'To-day is the funeral [of Herbert and Lloyd] at four o'clock, and I am going there myself in an hour. I assure you, my dear brother, I am the most unhappy man in the world. I shall never get

---

[1] King George to the Prince of Wales, 23 April 1870 *(Queen Victoria's Letters,* 2nd series, ed. Buckle, II, London, 1926, 15– 18): 'Many say the Opposition has made this coup (but without for an instant believing that this catastrophe would be the result) in order to discredit the government in the eyes of the public . . . I consider this likely.'

[2] Haymerle to Beust, 30 April 1870 (Bibliography no. 8): *'In seinem Unmuthe spricht er oft davon, das Land "aus dem nie etwas werden könne" zu verlassen.'*

over this all my life. How I pity poor Lord and Lady de Grey,
and Mr. Vyner's mother! I cry like a child when I think of this
. . . Please do not be angry with me if I write to you at this
moment, but I feel so very unhappy and desperate. Could you
express any words of regret to Lord de Grey for me? If you
think so, pray do! or perhaps it is better not. [1]

The bodies of Herbert and Lloyd had been put on board
the *Afróessa* on Thursday night and were brought into Piraeus
on Good Friday, 22 April. The funeral took place in Athens on
the following day. The coffins were carried up by rail to the
Monastiraki Station. Here they were covered with English
flags, and carried thence on the shoulders of English bluejack-
ets up Hermes Street and to the English Church in Philhel-
línon. An august assemblage waited to receive them. The service was read by the American pastor, Dr. Hill, who had acted
during many years as honorary chaplain to the English Legation. The congregation then went in procession to the Protestant cemetery, where the bodies were to lie. First walked Hill,
with two naval officers; then the king and Mr. Erskine; then
Lord Muncaster, who supported the weeping Mrs. Erskine; and
behind them came the diplomatic corps of Athens.

A few hours earlier the Swiss courier Gleissner, who had
been sent out by Erskine on the Friday to discover the as yet
uncertain fate of the younger captives, rode into the village of
Dilessi. He was guided to the house of a peasant, who conducted him inside a shed in his backyard. There, in two deal
boxes hastily nailed together, lay the bodies of Frederick Vyner
and Alberto de Boÿl. Gleissner went over to Vyner and looked
down at him with a pang of indescribable grief and pity. The
sweat and saliva caked thickly on the young man's cheeks and
jaws told of the fearful agony which had preceded his murder. But
his face was now perfectly tranquil and serene. The courier laid
his hand for a second on the cold forehead; and then he turned

[1] loc. cit.

away, to perform his last service for 'those gentlemen'. The bodies were soon placed on board ship and taken to Piraeus; and the obsequies in Athens followed, with the same gloomy solemnities, on Sunday, 24 April.

In the first moments of their revulsion the Greek public turned almost unanimously on the minister for war, General Soutzos. He was the minister responsible for the army and the rural gendarmerie, and it was his business to know the movements and to repress the activities of brigands and outlaws. But more than this: he owned large estates in Attica, both at Marathon and Tatoï.

As a landowner he regularly, and necessarily, paid blackmail to the brigands; and he was notoriously, though through no fault of his own, one of the principal *listapodóchoi*, or brigand-harbourers, in the country. That he had in fact known of the presence of the Arvanitákis gang in Attica before 11 April was indisputable.[1] But that he also knew of the excursion of Muncaster's party before that party's abduction was never proved, and appears on the face of it highly improbable. Public opinion, however, was in no mood to make fine distinctions. At the funeral of the murdered gendarme Vasilakos, which took place on 23 April, the public dissatisfaction was very palpably evinced by cries of 'Down with Soutzos!' At the funeral of Vyner on 24 April, the French minister Baron Baude observed Soutzos and said, in the hearing of Soutzos' brother, '*Il y a ici quelq'un de trop*', a sentiment shared by most of those present.[2] King George demanded and received Soutzos' resignation on 23 April, and was so deeply incensed that he could scarcely be persuaded, in his letter of acceptance, to append even the most frigid acknowledgment of the General's services. On learning from Erskine of Soutzos' connexion with Costa Seliamis, Lord Clarendon went so far as to propose that the General should be

[1] *Mellon,* 29 April 1870.
[2] Finlay to Mowbray Morris, 14 April 1870 (AG, 1870); Watbied 104.

taken up and examined as accessory, if not as an accomplice, to the murders.[1] But this was a false scent; and Soutzos was made to answer not so much for his own imperfections as for those of the Greek political system in general.

Abroad, in Austria, in France and in Turkey, the expectation that English troops would occupy Athens was universal: and such was the unpopularity of the Greek cause in those countries that most people also hoped they would. The Austrian Chancellor Beust told Lord Bloomfield that he was 'horror-struck', spoke of withdrawing his Minister from Athens, and promised his cooperation in all suitable measures. The French Ambassador in London, Lavalette, assured Clarendon that the Emperor's government would do whatever England liked whenever she desired it.

Of opinions in Turkey it is unnecessary to speak. The two exceptions to the prevailing current were the United States of America, then in the thick of their quarrel with England over the *Alabama,* and Russia, who for purposes of her own leapt forward as the eager and clamorous defender of Greece.

But in England the public indignation knew no bounds. The whole nation, press and public, Whig and Tory, seemed to have gone mad with rage and lust for revenge. With the honourable exceptions of the Liberal *Daily News* and the *Economist,* the newspapers vied with one another in heaping insults and menaces on the whole Greek nation, without regard to persons or parties. *The Times,* after a quick look over its shoulder, joined the hunt and was soon well up with the leaders of the pack. Greece was a disgrace to civilisation, a nest of robbers and pirates, a country of half-Slav, half-Greek demi-savages, the St. Giles's of Europe; 'every Greek is supposed to be a cheat and a swindler'; 'the only law observed in Greece is the law of pillage, the only king recognised is King Death'. Greece must be heavily punished, ruined, occupied by Indian troops, put under

[1] Clarendon to Erskine, 15 May 1870.

an English governor-general, handed back to Turkey, abolished and extirpated. It is impossible even now to read these tirades without sorrow and shame. The unreasoning prejudice in favour of Greece which had been so strong in 1821 had, after half a century, given way to an equally unreasoning prejudice against her. To explain the causes of this conversion would need a separate study; but the chief of them were two. The Protecting Powers, of which England was one, had in 1829 guaranteed the independence of Greece. Greece had repeatedly misused this guarantee to disturb the peace of the Eastern Mediterranean, with a view to expanding her frontiers at the expense of Turkey. If she succeeded, she expected to retain her spoils; if she failed, she relied on the guarantee of the Powers to protect her from Turkish reprisals. By 1870 England, whose cardinal policy in this area had been to preserve the integrity of the Othoman Empire as a barrier to Russian designs in the Near East, was exasperated by these continual attempts on the part of Greece to frustrate it. Moreover, the bland refusal of every Greek government to make the smallest attempt to pay the agreed interest on her loans was an affront to united Podsnappery, which saw at the same time vast fortunes being amassed, not always in the most scrupulous fashion, by Greek merchants in England and her Empire.

Yet it was not only anti-Greek feelings which inspired the public outcry at the Dilessi murders. There was also the first, to many acutely painful, sensation that England under Gladstone was not what she had been under Palmerston; and the realisation that the adorable species *civis britannicus* could now be hunted down and slain, apparently almost without protest, a bare five years after the death of its illustrious preserver. Nobody had any doubts what Lord Palmerston would have done. 'Palmerston', wrote the Austrian minister Haymerle, 'would certainly have fetched the fleet, instead of ordering back a squadron which happened to be on its way here. But

Lord Clarendon, at the first announcement, knew not what to do, except to telegraph that he thought the ransom exaggerated.'[1] Herbert's letter of 17 April to Erskine, in which he passed on the views of Takos, is from this point of view both touching and illuminating: 'I had better tell you what the chief says you ought to do, and you will judge how impracticable his views are. He says that the representatives of England and Italy should say to the Greek government that they do not care at all how the thing [the grant of amnesty] is done . . . but that all they require is the return of their people, *faute de quoi* the fleets of England and Italy will destroy Greece.' But were these views after all so impracticable? Were not the words of Takos, allowing for some floridity of expression, a fairly accurate summary of what England had, with far less excuse, done in 1850 and again in 1854, and of what many people in England believed she could do now in 1870? Those who saw that such an intervention would be not only criminal but also useless, were few indeed. 'If England', said Lord Carnarvon in the House of Lords, 'chooses to proclaim herself to the world as a second-rate Power, she must take the consequences. She must understand that all over the globe she will be taken at her word, and set down at the value at which she estimates herself.'[2]

For a moment it seemed that Mr. Gladstone's government might bow to the storm. On 27 April Admiral Sir Alexander Milne, the commander-in-chief at Malta, was instructed to divert to Crete the squadron which was proceeding on a good-will visit to Piraeus; and on 30 April the battleship *Royal Oak* was ordered to Salamis Bay: 'in case', Clarendon telegraphed to Erskine, 'you require assistance.' On 23 April Clarendon had summoned the Greek Minister in London, Mr. Vraïlas-Armenis, better known to the English as Sir Peter Braila, and had spoken with a severity such as to justiiy the gloomiest forebodings. 'In

[1] Haymerle to Beust, 30 April 1870 (Bibliography no.8).
[2] Official Report, 23 May 1870.

the end,' wrote Braila, 'he calmed down; but I have never seen him in such a rage, because, apart from everything else, he is suffering tortures from his gout.'[1] When on 27 April Erskine's dispatch of 16 April reached London, in which he told of Zaïmis' disclosure that the capture was being exploited by the political Opposition, Clarendon laid it before the Houses next day; and on 6 May he told Braila that the public resentment was such as he could never remember.[2] Clarendon had never approved of Palmerstonian methods of diplomacy: if he had, he could scarcely have served under Mr. Gladstone, who detested them. Yet it is plain that any strong move towards an active policy in Greece on the part of his colleagues would, at least in the last week of April, have had Clarendon's support.

But to the world's astonishment, no such move, indeed no move of any kind, was made. The voice of the nation, as it proclaimed itself in the press, was nearly unanimous. But there were exceptions: and the most important of these was the prime minister, Mr. Gladstone. He was sixty-one, and at the summit of his powers. He was the head of the strongest administration which had been in power for a generation, and his Liberal majority in the Commons was nearly one hundred and twenty.

His ascendancy over his colleagues was undoubted. He might, with not much exaggeration, have echoed the proud boast of the Father of gods and men in his own favourite poem:

> Ye strive in vain! If I but stretch this hand,
> I heave the gods, the ocean, and the land;
> For such I reign, unbounded and above;
> And such are men, and gods, compared to Jove.

The public clamour for revenge on Greece offended many of Gladstone's most cherished principles. In the first place, he

[1] Vraïlas-Armenis to Valaoritis, 23 April 1870 (Bibliography no. 18).
[2] Vraïlas-Armenis to Valaoritis, 10 May 1870 (ibid.).

disapproved of interference in the affairs of other nations, and above all he disapproved of the coercion of the weak by the strong. In the second place, he idolised democratic institutions, which any English intervention in Greece must suspend, if not finally destroy; no doubt the working of democracy in that country was faulty, but that was no reason for its modification, let alone its abolition. In the third place, his education and his experience had endeared Greece to him beyond other small nations. And lastly, military intervention might probably lead to bloodshed in an unjust cause: and, as he said in 1880, 'there is no war – except one, the war for liberty – that does not contain in it elements of corruption, as well as of misery, that are deplorable to recollect and to consider.' Twenty years before he had stood up manfully against Palmerston's bullying of Greece in the affairs of Finlay and Pacifico. Fourteen years later, much the same views were to dictate his refusal to intervene in the Sudan on behalf of General Gordon. The assaults on Greece of the Tory Lord Carnarvon and the Whig Lord Russell ('that buzzing little wasp at Pembroke Lodge'[1]) merely strengthened Mr. Gladstone's resolve that no material pressure of any kind should be put on that unhappy country. The louder the tempest roared, the firmer his resolution became. He dug in his heels, and refused to budge.

Mr. Gladstone's position was made clear at the outset. On 26 April Queen Victoria telegraphed from Osborne: 'The Queen has been deeply grieved at the terrible Greek tragedy. Will nothing be done to mark our indignation? Clearly the Greek Government are entirely answerable for what has occurred, and ought to make some reparation.' The cabinet met on the following day, and Gladstone put the Queen's telegram before them. 'Agreed', he noted laconically, 'that the amount of Greek responsibility is not yet ascertained';[2] and in that sense he replied to the Sovereign.

[1] Clarendon to Gladstone, 12 May 1870 (B.M. Add. 44134, fol. 199).
[2] Gladstone Papers, 27 April 1870 (B.M. Add. 44638, fol. 67).

This was all very well. But what was to be done? The public disturbance was such that wholly to ignore it would have been beyond any but the most autocratic government. In their tenderness for Greek democracy the English cabinet were in danger of outraging their own. In fairness even to Greece herself. whose nationals in England were suffering acutely, some chance should be given of justification and amendment. Mr. Maniakis, a Greek merchant of Manchester, wrote to *The Times* that 'the Marathon catastrophe has spread such consternation among the Greek residents of this city that I cannot even attempt to describe it.' The Greek merchants of London scarcely dared show their faces in the City.[1] The Athens newspapers were full of reports that Braila was a prisoner in his Legation, and that his windows had been smashed by raging mobs. And these reports, though destitute of any foundation, certainly arose from an accurate estimate of English public opinion.

First of all, there must be an Enquiry. Obviously there was much to be enquired into. Persons of high political importance in Greece were, according to the belief of both the king and his prime minister, involved in the affair; and Lord Clarendon was optimistic enough to believe that an enquiry might unmask them. 'The best proof of the sorrow of the Greek Government', he told Braila, 'will be found in the investigation of this atrocious crime being thorough, complete and sincere, in its disregard of persons of whatever category whom it may reach, and having for its sole object the truth.' Braila gave him an assurance that this would be so; and hastened to telegraph to Mr. Valaoritis that he really believed Lord Clarendon's hope for an impartial enquiry would be the extent of England's demands. He added, significantly but unnecessarily, that it would be a great scandal for Greece if it were believed that brigandage was an organ of political opposition.[2] No one in Greek political circles needed to be reminded of this.

[1] S A. Parasyrakis, *Panhellinion Himerologion,* 1880, 246.
[2] Vraïlas–Armenis to Valaoritis, 10 May 1870 (Bibliography no. 18).

On 28 April Clarendon commented thus on Erskine's dispatch of 16 April: 'This is a very serious matter . . . Mr. Zaïmis would scarcely have made to you the communication which he appears to have made without having some foundation for it.' And on 6 May, at the very start of the Enquiry, he instructed Erskine or his Secretary of Legation, Mr. Watson, to be present when witnesses were examined and to claim the right of cross-examination. It was here that the English government, in its turn, began to blunder and to transgress. Greek criminal procedure followed that of the Code Napoléon. According to this system, witnesses are examined initially by the juge d'instruction, and by him alone: *à huis clos*, as the phrase is. The only other persons who have a right to be present are the magistrate's clerk, who takes down the deposition and, if he so decides, the public prosecutor. All other persons, however deeply interested or involved in the case, are excluded. On the basis of the magistrate's report the prosecutor draws up his indictment and sends it forward to a consultative body known as the Chambre des mises en accusation, which, in its turn, either throws out the bill or commits the accused for public trial by jury. Whether the secrecy observed in the initial process be or be not more conducive to the discovery of truth than is the publicity of an English magistrates' court, was not the point at issue. Article 72 of the Greek Code of Criminal Procedure formally debarred both relatives and representatives of relatives of injured parties from participating in any instruction: and to demand the intervention of foreigners with power to cross-examine was a direct contravention of the law of the land. Why the English government, who had shown themselves so tender to the Greek Constitution over the amnesty, should have shown themselves so ruthless in violating the Greek Criminal Code, is one of the numerous puzzles to which no satisfactory answer can be found. They put and maintained themselves deliberately in the wrong, to no purpose whatever. The only result of their conduct was that, when the very absurd report of the Enquiry was finally published, the Greeks could, with some show of reason, claim that the English participants were as much responsible for it as they.

During the last days of April and the first days of May, Mr. Zaïmis and the public prosecutor, Mr. Limberákis, encouraged by the foreign minister, Mr. Valaoritis, tacitly allowed the intervention of Erskine and Watson, who were present at the examinations of the captured brigands, six in number, and of Alexander Anemoyiannis. But this could not last. The Enquiry soon assumed such proportions that neither Erskine nor Watson had time to follow it: and moreover neither of them knew any Greek. Erskine therefore asked for the assistance of an English lawyer to take over the work, and on 14 May Mr. Charles Cookson, the Legal Vice-Consul of the Supreme Consular Court in the Levant, together with his assistant, Mr. Edward Allan, arrived in Athens from Constantinople. The facilities accorded tacitly to Erskine could not be so transferred to those persons. The ablest lawyers in Greece, Provelengios, Saripolos and Damaskinos, the last of whom was legal adviser to the English Legation, all protested against the interference of Cookson and Allan. But Clarendon had taken the bit between his teeth, and Erskine, against his will,[1] was made to insist. The Greek government perforce gave way. On 19 May a secret agreement was drawn up and initialled by Erskine and the Greek minister of justice, Sarávas, which permitted the intevention of Cookson and Allan as 'witnesses' at all preliminary examinations so long as this privilege was exercised with as much discretion as might be, and not claimed as of right. The agreement was written out in duplicate and Erskine retained one copy of it. This

[1] Erskine to Granville 30 July 1870: 'All that has been hitherto done is not only humiliating to the Greek nation, but absolutely illegal....I will not conceal from Your Lordship that my own conviction all along has been that we had wrung from the Greek government a concession which they ought not to have made.'

was prudent: since, when the Zaïmis government fell in July, Mr. Sarávas went out of office with his own copy in his pocket. Cookson, a laborious but not very intelligent investigator, began his huge and hopeless task. But the irregularity of his position hung like a millstone about his neck. He repeatedly detected the prosecutor Limberákis in tampering with evidence which seemed to implicate political personages; 'but', he added, 'his position, as a legal functionary engaged daily in assisting foreigners to violate what all legal authorities consider one of the established principles of Hellenic criminal procedure, undoubtedly entitles him to great indulgence.'[1]

Under such discouraging auspices the Enquiry began. But at least it was a positive step, which could be cited in reply to the general taunt of the English public that 'nothing was being done'. However, the question which chiefly occupied the minds of the English government was not that of how the disaster had happened, but of why it should ever have happened at all.

The Greek Constitution of 1864 was on paper the most democratic in Europe. But it had been imposed, ready-made by theoreticians, on a people politically immature, whose notions of political activity were still confined within the age-old framework of patronage and coercion. The country was therefore governed in the only way in which such a country with such a constitution could be governed, that is to say, through bribery and violence exercised by unscrupulous party managers. To put the matter in its simplest terms: if a voter voted for his patron, he expected his *quid pro quo*; if he did not vote for him, he might probably get a *quid pro quo* of a less gratifying description. The fearful state to which the show of democratic institutions had brought the kingdom was mercilessly exposed by the brothers Vyzantios, who edited the newspaper *Iméra* from the safe distance of Trieste. In an article which was

---

[1] Cookson to Erskine, 16 June 1870.

widely copied and cited in Italian, French and English newspapers Alexander Vyzantios held up Greek ministers and parliamentary deputies alike to the scorn and obloquy of the world, and advocated in the plainest terms a radical revision of the Constitution, a drastic limitation of the franchise, and a conversion of the Crown from a plaything of the politicians into a supreme and effective instrument of administration.[1]

These views were fully shared by King George, who had been six years on the throne of Greece. On 4 May Sir Henry Elliot, the English ambassador in Constantinople, arrived in Athens and found the king still in the depths of despondency. To Erskine, His Majesty had been fairly discreet; but Elliot was an old friend and, as brother-in-law of Earl Russell, a personage of high standing and influence. To him the king spoke his mind with complete frankness. He entreated Elliot to represent to Lord Clarendon the impossibility of his continuing on the throne unless the friendly governments came to his assistance. He referred with special bitterness to the principal leaders of the Opposition, Messrs. Bulgaris and Koumoundouros, as 'the men who make all government impossible when they are in opposition, and bring the country to discredit when in power.' He said that 'without such an essential modification of the Constitution as should enable him to govern the country without leaving it at the mercy of the political intriguers who had reduced it to the present state, he did not see how he could continue to support the humiliation of his position.' Such a modification should be imposed by a fiat of the friendly Powers, and it would, he believed, be accepted with relief and alacrity by the Greek nation. Finally, he begged that what he had said should be regarded as 'most secret and confidential', since his own position would be untenable if he were known to have so spoken. Elliot was in an awkward situation. He fully sympathised with all that His Majesty had said; but he did not

[1] *L'Osservatore Triestino*, 16 May 1870; *Pall Mall Gazette*, 24 May 1870.

see how a constitutional government such as his own could possibly call for or support the suspension of a constitution elsewhere. The king repeated that this was now the only hope for Greece; and so the interview terminated.[1] Elliot next called in turn on the Opposition leaders, Mr. Bulgaris and Mr. Koumoundouros, and was disgusted by the selfishness and cynicism with which both of them spoke of the Dilessi murders. Each regarded the affair as a heaven-sent opportunity for turning out Mr. Zaïmis and reinstating himself. Elliot gave them a piece of his mind. He said, it was evident that not even the frightful tragedy which had brought disgrace on their nation was sufficient to make them forget their miserable rivalries and join for once, for the public good, in trying to put an end to an evil which they recognised as shameful, but by which each of them in turn endeavoured to profit. But what did they care for Sir Henry Elliot?[2]

It is possible that, had circumstances permitted, Lord Clarendon himself would have been ready to agree to some intervention on the lines indicated by King George. A long conversation which he had with Braila on 4 June merely confirmed the views expressed by the king to Elliot. After it, Clarendon wrote to Gladstone: 'I suppose that we, or *I* at all events, must pretend to think the Constitution good for Greece... but I am convinced that neither improvement or good government are [*sic*] possible under the present system which enables corrupt men to practise corruption with impunity.'[3] But to any such intervention there were two practical obstacles: the unshakable resolve of Mr. Gladstone, and the impossibility of any joint action on the part of the three Protecting Powers, England, France and Russia. France indeed would have been willing in principle to co-operate, but her

[1] Elliot to Clarendon, 9 May 1870.
[2] Ibid.
[3] Clarendon to Gladstone, 5 June 1870 (B.M. Add. 44134, fol. 216).

government was weak and the days of the Second Empire were numbered. Russia on the other hand was alarmingly, and significantly, hostile to England from the very start of the affair. On 14 May the English cabinet were still undecided as to what action, if any, could be taken; but on the following day the Tsar's government declared itself in a manner not to be mistaken.

It was Sunday afternoon. To Clarendon's surprise, the Russian ambassador, Baron Brunnow, was announced. The Baron began by speaking with emotion of his own recall from London, and of his distress at having to leave his 'adopted country'. But he soon broached the subject of the Greek imbroglio. He said, that his august Master felt deep anxiety on behalf of '*ce pauvre petit Roi*', King George; and he handed Clarendon a letter from the Russian Chancellor, Prince Gortchakow, which, though not unfriendly in tone, gave a plain warning that Russia would not tolerate, far less assist in, any English intervention in Greece. Clarendon saw at once that any such idea must be abandoned. He borrowed Gortchakow's letter to send to Gladstone, and added, 'It shows that we may easily get into *complications* with Russia about Greece, and that we must be very careful in our proceedings.'[1] Next day Gortchakow summoned Mr.Dragoumis, the Greek chargé at Petersburg, and told him that he had acted energetically on Greece's behalf with the government in London, '*à qui Brunnow a dit ce qu'il faut.*'[2] That autocratic Russia should have come forward to defend unbridled democracy in Greece against an assumed intention of democratic England to suppress it, provides an amusing instance of the unscrupulousness of power politics.

How Mr. Disraeli and Lord Derby would have reacted to this hardly veiled menace, is a question. It is clear that Lord Clarendon was thoroughly upset by it. He was, in fact, a dying

---

[1] Clarendon to Gladstone, 15 May 1870 (B.M. Add. 44134, fol. 202).
[2] L. Héritier, 329 and note 1.

man: he had the gout in both feet, and felt 'altogether ill'. Full debates on the murders were down, in the Commons for Friday, 20 May, and in the Lords for Monday, 23 May. The cabinet at their meeting on 7 May had deprecated this public discussion as premature; and, after Brunnow's visit, Clarendon very heartily concurred in this opinion. He was, he said, convinced that discussion at that moment could do no good, and might be very harmful and embarrassing. A violent reaction would be provoked among political circles in Athens; but the real danger lay not so much in Athens as in St. Petersburg: 'indeed, there is no foretelling what the mischief in the East might be if Russia, under pretence of protecting the King, were to take sides against us in Greece.'[1]

But, however premature and embarrassing it might be, discussion could not be avoided. In truth, the public excitement was such that not even Gladstone's influence could induce the promoters of the Commons debate to withdraw, even though both proposer and seconder sat on the benches behind him. The Lords debate was of course demanded by Herbert's cousin, Carnarvon, who enjoyed great popular sympathy and was entitled to every indulgence. Gladstone bowed to the inevitable and managed the affair with all the address of an old parliamentary hand. All through Friday the business of the House dragged on. It was after midnight when Sir Roundell Palmer rose to open the discussion on the murders; and well past two in the morning when the prime minister rose to reply. At first all went well for the government. Palmer was diffuse and legalistic, spending much time on the untenable proposition that Herbert, as a diplomatic agent of Her Majesty's Government, was the legal responsibility of the Greek government wherever he might be or whatever he might be doing. A more formidable antagonist followed, in the person of Sir Henry Lytton Bulwer. Bulwer had begun life as a philhellene; but a

[1] Clarendon to Gladstone, 18 May 1870 (B.M. Add. 44134, fol. 205).

long career in the diplomatic service, which had ended with a not very prosperous tenure of the embassy at Constantinople, had modified his youthful enthusiasm for Greece. He had also been the intimate friend of Edward Herbert. He now assailed the Greek government with unmeasured ferocity. He made against them the inexcusable charge that their sudden display of energy in sending out the troops had been due to a realisation that they would be called on to pay the ransom: a charge not only false, but also palpably absurd. As for Colonel Theagenis, their agent, he was as much the murderer of the unhappy captives as if he had shot them dead with his own hand, which would have been a more merciful course. Bulwer was on firmer ground in ridiculing the farce of democratic institutions in Greece: and here King George, his foreign minister Valaoritis, and his minister in London, Braila, to name only three, would have concurred. He demanded the imposition of law and order in that country; and ended by proposing an amendment which, if it had been pressed to a division and carried, would have committed the government to a condemnation of the Greek ministers and to 'concerting with their Allies as to the best means of establishing in Greece a Government capable of satisfying the ordinary requirements of a civilised state': which amounted to a pledge of active intervention.

At this crisis the prime minister was all himself. It is difficult nowadays to understand the influence which Mr. Gladstone's rhetoric exerted on his hearers. Animated no longer by that 'voice of singular fullness', that 'falcon's eye, that 'great actor's command of gesture', his speeches seem to lose themselves in a wilderness of turgid inelegancies; and his passion for qualification and parenthesis was such as make many of his statements nearly meaningless to a modern reader. In the piling clausulae one seems to detect the accents, not so much of Cicero, as of his pupil Dr. Blimber. But at least this instrument was well fitted for the task now in hand – that of saying as little as possible at great length and with great elaboration.

The whole matter, said Mr. Gladstone, was most obscure; most difficult to pronounce on at this stage. The more one looked into it, the deeper the complications became. At one point his cumbrous vehicle seemed to have rolled itself to the edge of the abyss; that is to say, to a point where some definite promise for action was inevitable. He spoke of the clandestine relations which 'appeared' to have prevailed between the brigands and political parties in Athens. 'It is at this point,' he went on, 'that we seem to touch on what connects this melancholy tragedy with defects of political and social organization that lift it altogether out of the category of a common and isolated occurrence, and make it a question entailing the necessity . . .' of what? of some course of action? but no: 'entailing the necessity of a deeper insight, if we can attain to it, than we have ever yet possessed, into the true interior condition of Greek society and Greek statesmanship.'

In two of his rare flashes of illumination Mr. Gladstone's position was revealed. He deplored his right honourable friend's attack on the popular institutions of Greece. And he made it as clear as his language could make anything that the English government contemplated no punitive intervention of any kind: 'There are two lines of action – that which is to heal the wounded feelings and possibly stay the rising resentment of the British nation; and that line of action is parallel with and immediately neighbouring to another line of action which would result in the measures required for the safety, honour and happiness of Greece. Whatever attains this latter end will also attain the former. It is a consolation in these circumstances to think that there are no selfish purposes to pursue, no vengeful purposes, because the condition of Greece is such as to make it impossible that she should be, in the body of her people, a fitting object of punishment for the miscarriages or misconduct of her government, provided we find ourselves in a condition to be able to obtain that best reparation which would consist in securities against the recurrence of similar evils.' He hoped that his right honourable friend would withdraw his amendment. His right honourable friend did so; and the House adjourned for the week-end at three o'clock on Saturday morning.

The Lords' debate was remarkable for the severity, understandable in the circumstances, of Lord Carnarvon's attack on Greece; and for a brief intervention on the part of the almost legendary figure of Lord Stratford de Redcliffe. He who, at an age when many young men were still writing Latin hexameters and making love to their bed-makers' daughters, had been left in sole charge of his country's interests at Constantinople, and had there negotiated a Russo-Turkish treaty which had freed a strong Russian army for the purpose of repelling Napoleon from Moscow, glanced with scarcely veiled contempt at the pitiful doings of Erskine. 'I do not say', he said, 'that everything was done by Mr. Erskine precisely as I might myself have advised.' Certainly not. But what Lord Stratford would have advised was unfortunately no longer practicable in 1870. Yet his apprehension of what England should do with respect to Greece was, even at that hour, much clearer than that of most of his countrymen. Few realised as he did that the status of a Protecting Power was obsolete, and that it should either be a reality or altogether abandoned. When the debate was resumed on 11 July 1870, Lord Stratford put the alternatives very plainly; either an English fleet should be stationed during five or even ten years at Piraeus, an English minister be included in the Greek government, and vigorous military reforms be introduced for the rooting out of brigandage; or else England should withdraw and take no further responsibility of any kind for Greece. 'But I see', he added, 'by the faces of the occupants of the Treasury Bench that they have made up their minds to do nothing.' He was quite right.

To do nothing! But what was there to do? This was the cabinet's problem. A way out of the dilemma seemed to be offered in a dispatch of the Athens correspondent of *The Times*, George Finlay, which appeared in that newspaper on 19 May:

> The Protecting Powers [he wrote] know better than the Greeks themselves what are the defects and abuses of the Hellenic administration, and it is not an act of interference in the government of the country to point out in diplomatic memorials what are the abuses and defects which require a remedy. That remedy the Greeks and their government must be left to find for themselves, but the British Government can publish its advice and ask the Greek Government to furnish it with information on the progress that has been made in reforming the different branches of the public administration.

This was scarcely more than a straw, but Gladstone clutched at it. He suggested that Lord Clarendon should send for Braila, explain that the cabinet were in a quandary over the Greek question, and ask for Braila's own views on what should be done.

Clarendon needed no second bidding. On 4 June he opened his whole heart to Braila, and his tone, conciliatory and almost apologetic, would have moved the large majority of Englishmen to yet more terrible paroxysms of indignation and fury. 'Without reserve,' he wrote to Gladstone, 'I told him [Braila] all our difficulties—the pressure of public opinion at home that *something should be done* in Greece—the desire of the Protecting Powers [he referred presumably to England and France] to strengthen the king's hands by modifying the Constitution—our determined resistance to coup d'état and foreign imposition of new institutions —on the other hand our determination for the good of peace to put down brigandage if possible, and our doubts whether this could be effected by Greek instrumentality, though we wished not to resort to any others etc., etc.' It is not surprising that Braila should have been nonplussed by this hesitant and self-contradictory approach. He admitted that no country 'could improve or even *stand on its legs* with universal suffrage, a single Chamber, a puppet King, and no public opinion or education to serve as a check on universal corruption'. The leaders of the Opposition, Bulgaris and Koumoundouros, he stigmatised with complete frankness as 'rogues'; but he noted that together they commanded a great majority of the parliamentary deputies.[1] The tenor of Braila's opinion clearly was that nothing could be done except by force: and to the use of force both Mr. Gladstone and the Tsar Alexander were, each for different reasons, unalterably opposed.

Now, if not before, the English government should have realised that the game was up. They should have abandoned all thought of reform by advice and consent of Greek politicians; have sent Cookson and Allan back by the first available steamer to Constantinople; have recalled Erskine to London; and have thrown up the pretence of their 'protection' of the Greek kingdom. So much was seen clearly enough by Lord Stratford de Redcliffe. By persisting in their courses the English government could do nothing but make England the laughing-stock and show of Greece and Europe; and that, too, at a time when it was vital for the cause of European peace that she should appear strong and effective. But the cabinet thought they knew better. Despite the discouragement of Braila, Erskine was instructed on 13 June to make the same cordial and conciliatory approach to Mr. Zaïmis and his colleagues, with a view to eliciting their views on the necessary reforms.

Erskine had at least sense enough to see that this plan of action—if such it could be called—was perfectly useless. Messrs. Zaïmis, Delyannis, Avyerinós and Sarávas he knew to be 'unscrupulous politicians, differing only in the degree of their selfishness': these men, he predicted would propose no reforms,

[1] Clarendon to Gladstone, 5 June 1870 (B.M. Add. 44134, fol. 213).

since they would never admit that, under their administration, there was anything to reform. 'They will probably reply', said Erskine, with a rare touch of humour, 'that although the late tragic occurrence at Dilessi has occasioned them some embarrassment, it must not be supposed that the internal condition of the Kingdom is such as to justify alarm.'[1] But Mr. Zaïmis prudently declined to give any answer at all.

Erskine then turned, with better hope, to the Greek foreign minister. Here the English government met with the single stroke of good fortune which attended them throughout the affair: for the foreign minister was Spyridon Valaoritis, cousin of the celebrated poet. Valaoritis was a native of the Ionian Islands. He had served the English Protectorate well in the Corfu senate, and had been rewarded with a K.C.M.G. At the Union of the Islands with Greece in 1864 he had migrated to Athens and entered Greek politics, resigning his foreign title, except in the eyes of the Ionian Bank, to which he was and remained Sir Spyridion Valaority. His western manners and anglophil proclivities were distrusted by the Athenian politicians and press; but his ability and integrity were undoubted, and he was known to be King George's *homme de confiance*. It was at the king's request that in January 1870 Valaoritis had become foreign minister. The appointment was naturally unpopular with the opposition newspapers, which sneered at him as 'the gentleman'. If by this appellation they meant to convey that he was possessed of certain qualities inimical to success in Greek public life, they were certainly right. The English administration at Corfu, whatever its faults, had for obvious reasons had no recourse to fraud or corruption: and Valaoritis had been profoundly disturbed and disgusted by the political methods which he found to be prevalent in Greece. Had he been better acquainted with nineteenth-century – not to speak of eighteenth-century – England, he might have found less to

---

[1] Erskine to Clarendon, 15 June 1870.

shock him at Athens. At all events, he was determined to do what he could, short of political suicide, to expose the whole miserable system of which Dilessi had been the latest and most terrible product. And when Mr. Erskine applied to him for help, he willingly agreed to provide it, with the sole proviso that he should not be cited as the source of the information he had to give. A few days later he placed in Erskine's hands, for transmission to Mr. Gladstone's new foreign secretary, Lord Granville,[1] a bulky memorandum on the nature and causes of the internal disorders of Greece. He listed the one hundred and nine chief cases of brigandage that had occurred during the past eighteen months. Like the brothers Vyzantios, he placed the responsibility for the organisation and protection of brigandage squarely on the shoulders of the political chiefs, the deputies, and their local and municipal officials. And he ended with a full catalogue of the names of those in political life who were most notorious as exploiters and patrons of these outlaws.[2]

The arrival in London, on 22 July, of this extraordinary document must have created in the Foreign Office a sensation such as for the moment to eclipse even the Franco-Prussian War. 'Better not print,' minuted Mr. Hammond; but he circulated it to the Queen, Mr. Gladstone and the appropriate Foreign Office departments. And the impression created on the mind of the English government by this factual analysis from the pen of the Greek foreign minister himself, fortified as it was by the opinions both of King George and of his prime minister Zaïmis, was such that no amount of denial, protest and vituperation in the Greek Parliament and press could ever efface it.[3]

For, meantime, an at first sight ludicrous conflict had been raging between Mr. Zaïmis and his political opponents. It will be recalled that on 15 April Zaïmis had, in conversation with

[1] Lord Clarendon died on 27 June 1870; Lord Granville became foreign secretary on 6 July.
[2] See Appendix, below p.174.
[3] Cf. Granville to Stuart, 1 May 1871.

Erskine, stated his belief that 'leading members of the Opposition' had been trafficking with the Arvanitákis gang on the previous night; and he had added that Takos, though convinced that the amnesty could be given, had sent to Athens to consult 'three advocates of standing' as to the legal position. The publication of Erskine's dispatch in which this conversation had been reported, was bound to cause trouble in Athens. The dispatch was laid before the English Parliament on 28 April. Two days later, rumours of its fateful contents were filtering into Greece by way of Trieste. On 5 May the whole text was available: and the full storm burst over the head of Mr. Zaïmis.

Now, there is no doubt at all that Erskine had faithfully recorded what Zaïmis had said to him; or that, at least as regarded the 'advocates of standing', Zaïmis had spoken the truth.[1] He admitted this in private to Erskine on 10 May:

> He [Zaïmis] did not deny that he had spoken to me of his conviction that this affair was being turned to account for party purposes, adding however that . . . he had a right to expect that [his suspicions] would not be made public . . . It would be impossible, he continued, for any public man to speak openly to a foreign minister on such terms. The publication of my despatch had already raised such a storm of indignation against him on the part of the Opposition that the difficulties of his position had become all but insuperable.[2]

The Opposition parties deputed three prominent politicians to write to Zaïmis demanding an explanation. The legal profession also was up in arms, and wrote letters of protest both to Zaïmis and to Erskine. Zaïmis, under this pressure, concocted and put out a fictitious version of his conversation with Erskine: he had been quite misunderstood by the English minister; what he had really said was that some persons had intervened

[1] Cookson to Erskine, 14 July 1870: '. . . Evidence has turned up confirming by the most undoubted testimony the fact . . . that the brigands actually did send an emissary to Athens a day or two after the capture . . . to ask the opinion of at least one well-known Athenian lawyer as to the possibility of obtaining an amnesty.' The lawyer was Ep. Louriotis (Cookson to Erskine, 4 February 1871).
[2] Erskine to Clarendon, 11 May 1870.

'out of a spirit of opposition to the government', a clause which might be taken as referring to the criminal classes in general, which were by definition opposed to all governments indifferently. He begged Erskine to approve this revised account of what had passed between them. But Erskine, though he regretted the publication of his dispatch nearly as deeply as did Mr. Zaïmis, could not bring himself to countenance so bare-faced a falsehood. He would go so far as to write a letter explaining that by 'leading members of the Opposition' he had not understood Mr. Zaïmis to mean the actual party leaders personally; and he left it at that. This did not satisfy the Opposition, which wrote a second protest to the prime minister. But this remained unanswered. After all, what more was there to say?

The interest of this violent and enduring controversy lies in the paradox that the opinion expressed by Mr. Zaïmis to Mr. Erskine on 15 April corresponded absolutely with what everyone else in Athens was saying and believing to be true; and yet that its publication abroad could release such an avalanche of resentment, expostulation and denial. The explanation of this paradox is to be sought very near to the heart of nineteenth-century Greek life: and without some brief comment on it, neither the Dilessi affair itself, nor the quarrel over the 'leading members', nor the results of the official Enquiry, can be wholly intelligible to a foreign reader a century after these events.

# CHAPTER SIX

# TRUTH AND 'ETHNIC' TRUTH

If any of my readers set out with the notion that all races
of men act and think much in the same way as educated
English-men . . . this work should suffice to disabuse him of
so erroneous a prepossession.

SIR JAMES GEORGE FRAZER

The Greek of the nineteenth century was a man who, like his
Byzantine ancestor, lived simultaneously on two levels of consciousness. There was the level of factual, observed truth, on
which he had to conduct his everyday life. And there was the
upper level of ideal truth, on which he claimed to appear in the
eyes of the outside world. These levels of truth seldom
approached one another, and were often sharply divergent: and
this led to a dichotomy in the Greek mind which contemporary, secularised Europe could not understand at all, and attributed, rather unfairly, to an inherent deceitfulness of character.

The factual, observed truth about Greek politics in the
third quarter of the nineteenth century was somewhat as follows. The Greek kingdom occupied a small territory in the
south of the Balkan Peninsula, much of which was mountain-
ous and infertile. Its independence from Turkey hung on the
guarantee of three powerful nations, Britain, France and Russia, who were known as the Protecting or Benefactory Powers.
Its inhabitants numbered less than two millions. They were
thrifty and intelligent, with a love of learning and culture
unparalleled among their neighbours. Yet their whole system of
government was radically vicious. Their state was, constitution-
ally, democratic; but, owing to its political immaturity, its

democracy was stultified by the organised tyranny of political parties. The Constitution of 1864 had curtailed the powers of the Crown and abolished the Upper Chamber; and the whole country was held fast in a system of corruption and intimidation manipulated by four or five powerful party managers. These men held their precarious and ephemeral terms of office by attaching to themselves a nucleus of parliamentary deputies, by a liberal distribution of 'places' to their supporters in the towns, by appointing their friends to be 'nomarchs' and 'eparchs' over the provinces and counties, and by securing, if necessary by force, the election of their nominees as 'demarchs' or mayors in the rural municipalities. Even the demarch was thus a mere party hack, whose first loyalty was not to the district which had been bullied or bribed into electing him, but to his political faction in Athens. The power of the nomarch, or lord-lieutenant, was great. He disposed of wide local patronage. He apportioned the taxes to be raised in his province. He could, and often did, override the decisions of his local councils by simple reference to the all-powerful minister of the interior, from whom he depended. And he and his subordinates had naturally endless opportunities of vexing and oppressing their political opponents, especially in regard to the collection of the tithe exacted on all agricultural produce.

In this web of political intrigue everybody down to the humblest peasant was enmeshed. Deputies and nomarchs and mayors, and their enemies who hoped to oust and succeed them, bound to themselves and their factions every family in the land, by ties far stronger than those of mere political affinity: by ties of fear, or self-interest, or even of spiritual relationship. Many were the spiritual kin, the 'gossips', of their supporters; and this 'gossipred' implied reciprocal obligations. To be the 'man' of the deputy or demarch was both to support and to be supported by him through thick and thin. The spiritual tie assured the performance of these undertakings: the powerful gossip protected his spiritual brother or son from oppression, and he in turn became the gossip's steady political supporter, which, under a system of universal adult suffrage, was no light matter. These affiliations were of course widely known: and the secrecy of the ballot was, at least in the rural districts, an open secret.

In a state of affairs in which everything was decided solely on grounds of party advantage by powerful cliques in Athens, the economic and social interests of the countryside naturally came a very poor second best. The principal occupation of Greece was agriculture. It was in crying need of modern agricultural equipment, of roads, of internal security, and of an equitable taxation. But the money required for these improvements was never forthcoming: it was needed for the party purposes of buying supporters and of creating more and more 'places' and sinecures—in the ministries, in civil life, in the armed forces—which these supporters could retain so long as their party remained in power, and might hope to resume when that power was regained.

The aim of every party was power alone: simply to be in office and in control of the machine.[1] No differences in programmes or policies divided them. The single purpose in the political field was the Great Idea, that is to say, the territorial expansion of Greece at the expense of the Othoman Empire; and in this purpose all parties were at one. The Great Idea held an unbounded sway over the mind of every Greek, and its vigorous prosecution, however untimely and inept, was enough to secure a measure of popularity for the most corrupt and self-seeking politician. No party had the smallest interest in any internal reform or development, and all regarded with the keenest suspicion and jealousy any foreign enterprise which seemed to promise a successful exploitation of the country's resources. The dislike of foreigners was in fact universal: they

[1] Prince Nicholas, 76.

were unpleasant necessities, to be spied upon, flattered or defamed as occasion offered.

The party struggle was carried on from day to day with a violence and rancour, an unscrupulousness and irresponsibility, unexampled elsewhere in nineteenth-century Europe. When one party obtained office, the rest instantly united, in defiance of all consistency or principle, to dislodge it. The press, which boasted seventy-seven separate newspapers, was free. Each party controlled a group of these newspapers, which devoted most of their space to vilifying and calumniating its political opponents very much in the style of the *Eatanswill Gazette* and the *Eatanswill Independent*. The wildest accusations were bandied about from side to side, without regard to truth or decency. The party chiefs were often honourable and stainless in their private lives, yet capable of devising or sanctioning any means, not excluding murder, to achieve their political ends. 'Their basic principle', as their contemporary Alexander Vyzantios very truly said of them, 'is that the notions of honour and decency prevailing in private life have no relevance to politics.'

To reign as king over this unhappy state had been chosen, seven years previously, a young fellow of eighteen, a foreigner, wholly western in manners and upbringing. He was, naturally enough, all at sea. The party leaders exploited and overreached him by turns, and his helplessness was the jest of the very outlaws who ravaged his kingdom. He could indeed dismiss his advisers and send for others; but of what use was that, when there was not one of them to mend another? 'I am now,' he said to Sir Henry Elliot, 'absolutely powerless among a set of men whose political conduct is only guided by their personal interests and a wish to acquire power. The elections are mere delusions, and managed both by intrigue and by the actual intimidation of brigands.'[1]

[1] Elliot to Clarendon, 9 May 1870; cf. Aspréas, II, 15.

It was not surprising that such men should have made full use of brigandage as a political weapon. The chief reason why brigandage was not seriously challenged until 1870 was not the impossibility of suppressing an evil artfully fostered by Turkish intriguers across the border, but rather the inconvenience of dispensing with it as a means of intimidation at home. At the times of elections, both parliamentary and municipal, the party which could call in the aid of brigands or outlaws was the party which was found to head the poll; and no amount of care in superintending the ballot could be of avail where whole bodies of electors were deterred by musket-balls from reaching the polling-stations.[1] But the employment of brigands, like the assumption of 'gossipred', involved a reciprocal obligation. Patronage, harbouring and protection of brigands were nearly universal among the chief men of every country district. These men were, to use the Italian term, *Maffiosi*. They paid a heavy blackmail. They turned a blind eye on the freelance activities of their protégés: on kidnapping and extortion and on the most atrocious cruelties. They intervened to secure the release of any of 'their' brigands who was unlucky enough to be taken and convicted. And there is ample evidence to show that the efforts of the military to surround and overpower gangs so protected were, as often as not, frustrated by political pressure exerted on both officers and men. The nomarch of the province of Acarnania, Mr. Zygomalas, told the English vice-consul at Missolonghi, Mr. Blakeney, that the troops employed against brigands in his area were useless for the task, since their officers belonged to a faction hostile to the government of the day. Blakeney's report of this conversation was published, and the usual protests followed, and the inevitable *démenti* on the part of the nomarch. But there is not the slightest doubt that he had so spoken to Mr. Blakeney, or that he had spoken truly.[2]

[1] Anon., *Those Responsible*: a fearful indictment of Peloponnesian nomarchs.
[2] Blakeney to Erskine, 11 May, 20 June 1870.

The army itself was in a deplorable state of inefficiency. Its strength according to the pay-roll was 13,865. But from this total could be deducted at least 4,000 as 'dead men' who existed only on paper. Colonel Koronaios, appointed in 1869 to root out brigandage in Acarnania, complained that the war minister Soutzos could never, or would never, put even one thousand effectives at his disposal; although Finlay calculated that at least that number of uniformed men sat eight hours a day in the coffee-shops of Athens: that five hundred more were enrolled as servants: and that the idle garrison of the capital, commanded by General Soutzos' brother, outnumbered that of Edinburgh.[1] The rural gendarmerie of Attica and the Megarid was chronically under strength, and one officer resigned in protest at having to discharge with twenty men duties which required ten times that number. The truth was that the largest part of the military were the mere salaried hangers-on of the political parties. The few determined and able soldiers, such as were Colonel Koronaios or Captain Liakopoulos or—whatever his enemies might say—General Soutzos himself, were powerless in face of the universal corruption and incompetence.

This then, or something very like this, was the factual truth about Greek political life in 1870. But it would of course be misleading to judge it by the standards of the twentieth century. It was not necessary to go back many years to find a state of affairs almost as disreputable in England. Edmond About himself, by no means eager to excuse the Greeks of any fault or failing he had noted in them, traced the political methods of his brigand chief Hadgi-Stavros to a visit paid by him to a parliamentary election in a Yorkshire rotten borough, which had 'filled him with deep reflexions on constitutional government, and on the profits to be made from it.'[2] Even after the Reform Act, intimidation was frequent at parliamentary elections, a fact

[1] Finlay to Mowbray Morris, 14 April 1870 (AG 1870).
[2] About, *Le Roi des montagnes,* 27.

which that savage persecutor of Greece in 1870, Sir Henry Bulwer, would have done well to remember. At the Coventry election of 1832 the Whig managers hired a gang of roughs who knocked down, kicked and stripped every Tory elector who approached the hustings. The two Whig candidates were naturally victorious: and one of them was Henry Bulwer.[1] Intimidation of men by masters, and the open purchase of votes, were common until the introduction of the ballot in 1870. The personal characters of the English party leaders during the '70s were doubtless superior to those of their Greek contemporaries, as they were to those of Walpole and the Pelhams. But among the general run of members of parliament were to be found many as unscrupulous as Koumoundouros or as corrupt as Delyannis.[2] It would have been nothing short of miraculous if Greece, after a bare half-century of independence and a bare six years of a constitution the most democratic in Europe, should already have emancipated herself from the abuses to which such constitutional liberty is at first inevitably exposed. And if responsible Greeks had frankly admitted the prevalence of such abuses, and asked for the help of the Powers in putting an end to them, such help would readily have been supplied. But this was the one admission which no Greek who wished to prosper, or even to live, in any Greek community could afford to make.

For the myth, the upper level of truth, reflected a different order. It was informed by the transcendent and mystical concept of the Nation, the 'ethnos', a term which comprehended everybody inside or outside the little kingdom who was of, or wished to claim, Hellenic descent. According to the 'ethnic' truth, the modern Greek was at once the spiritual heir of all the

[1] Norman Gash, *Politics in the Age of Peel* (London, 1953), 148– 9.
[2] 'M. Delyanni being, in my opinion, one of the worst and most corrupt specimens of a public man to be found even in Greece'; Erskine to Clarendon, 15 June 1870.

splendid intellectual endowments of the classical age, and the political heir of all the vast pretensions, both religious and imperial, of Byzantium. From the first of these he derived his genius and culture, from the second his natural right and fitness to resume the Empire over all the nations of the eastern Mediterranean; and from both his evident superiority, in intellect and capacity, over the members of any other race. It followed from these premises that his conduct was above reproach, and his country a paragon of order and enlightenment. He was acutely conscious of the importance of persuading the outside world of these truths, deeply grateful to any observer who proclaimed them, and fiercely resentful of any kind of criticism which seemed to belie them. The inescapable paradox of his position lay in the fact that his own politicians and newspapers were daily heaping on one another abuse far more damaging than any which could have been devised by an outsider.[1] But the internal dissensions of his country were, he felt, a matter for himself, and of no concern to anybody else. The torrent might run confused and polluted below, but the bright rainbow remained steady and shimmering above it. The business of the world in general was to fix its gaze on and adore the insubstantial halo. Anybody who directed the world's attention downwards to the material but muddy cataract was, if he were a Greek, a traitor and blasphemer, and if he were a foreigner, a 'mis-hellene'.

The term 'mis-hellene', or Greek-hater, with its correlative 'phil-hellene', or Greek-lover, demands a word of explanation. The best account of it was written, shortly after this time, by the ingenious Angelos Vlachos, who declared it to be a unique phenomenon in contemporary thought. By the Greek of his times, Vlachos tells us, the whole of humanity was divided into two groups, the Greek-lovers and the Greek-haters. The latter

[1] 'It would be a great misfortune if ever Europe were to base its opinions on such a Greek Press as this': *Aión,* 19 May 1870.

group was, unfortunately, by far the larger, since it included not only adverse critics of Greece but also that considerable portion of the human family which knew nothing about her or had never heard of her: and this ignorance or indifference was in itself a crime against the Hellenic 'ethnos'. The adverse critics who qualified as 'mis-hellenes' were not only such confirmed and malicious calumniators as Edmond About and George Finlay, but also those who had expressed dissatisfaction or scepticism of any kind at all; and the majority of these would have been surprised, Vlachos said, to learn that they had been baptised haters of Greece by that country. The contemporary Greek-lovers, on the other hand, were those who, however ignorantly, accepted the 'ethnos' at its own valuation and published their views abroad. These were, without exception, men of the highest intelligence, discernment and integrity.

This rigid segregation of humanity into sheep and goats was in origin religious: for the concept of Hellenism was inextricably fused, in Greece as in Byzantium, with that of Orthodox Christianity. In the Byzantine mind there was, on earth as in heaven, but one empire and one faith. The emperor of the day was the temporal image and vice-gerent of Jesus Christ. Those who subscribed to his power and pretensions, and to the Greek culture and supremacy of his universal realm, were the only true Christians. Those who owed allegiance to spiritual or temporal powers outside it were either pagans or heretics, and fell under the general head of barbarians or 'gentiles'. In brief, the Greek empire of Byzantium was that kingdom of God upon earth for which Christ had taught His disciples to pray; and he that was not with it was automatically against it. Belief in the divine sanction accorded to their mission and in the divine decree that one day that mission would be fulfilled had never died away in the hearts of the Greeks, and it recrudesced with vigour in the new kingdom. From it derived that moral stigma attaching to critics of the 'ethnos', who were guilty not merely of malice but also of blasphemy. It is entirely in accordance with this conception that when the 'ethnos' was attacked by foreigners, the imagery to which its defenders instinctively resorted was that of Christ's Passion. The Greek saw his 'ethnos' spat upon and scourged and nailed to a cross; and he looked on with eyes overflowing with self-pity and a heart bursting with resentment against those who could so sin against the pattern of divine innocence and majesty. The assaults on Greece in the foreign press over the Dilessi affair called forth much of this imagery in her defence: and it was unkind in a French newspaper to point out that those who had been done to death were in fact not Greeks at all, and to enquire, since the analogy had been drawn, who was cast for the rôle of the Penitent Thief?

The 'ethnic' myth constituted a canon of infallible truth: and this canon was constantly growing. Once the 'ethnos' had ruled on any event, its pronouncement became an article of faith which none but the most obstinate and bad-hearted would question. Heretics there doubtless were, even in Greece herself, such as Andreas Laskaratos and Spyridon Valaoritis and the poet Dionysios Solomós;[1] but most of these came, significantly enough, from the Ionian Islands, which had for centuries been open to western modes of thought. The overwhelming mass of the population subscribed unquestioningly to the canon; and those who aspired to success in public life did so of necessity.

This brief account,[2] of the double standard of truth prevailing in Greece at that time may help us to understand how it came about that things which everybody knew to have happened, and to be happening daily, could at the same time never

[1] '*La nazione deve considerare come nazionale ciò che è vero*' (Solomós).
[2] Derived from many contemporary sources: Tuckerman, pp. 329–66, a favourable witness, is illuminating, as is Senior, pp. 354 ff.; though neither was aware of the specifically Byzantine element in Greek thought.

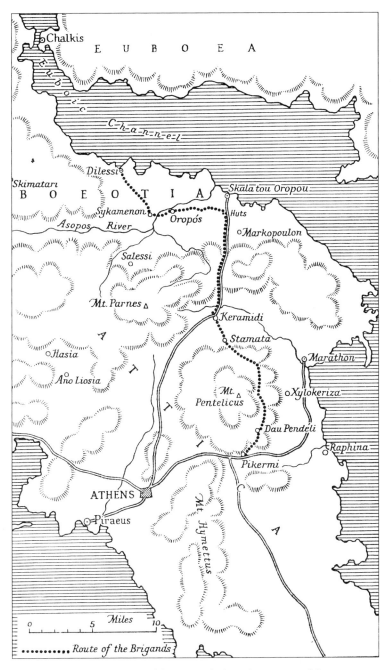

Map illustrating the route of the Brigands from the capture of the party at
Pikermi on 11 April to the murders at Dilessi on 21 April 1870

Edward Herbert                    Frederick Vyner

King George of the Hellenes          Thrasyvoulos Zaïmis

Church at Oropós, attended by the Greek Brigands and their prisoners

House of Mr. Skourtaniotis at Oropós where the hostages were confined

The trial of the brigands in Athens. Colonel Theagenis is giving evidence

have happened at all. Those unfamiliar with the historical factors which gave rise to the 'ethnic' standard may find the account strange, and be tempted to think it exaggerated. Yet it is far from being so. Two brief examples may be cited to prove this. One of the many defenders of his country in the Dilessi affair was a Mr. Evangelos Arniotákis, who, in a pamphlet entitled *The Voice of Greece* and printed at Smyrna in 1871, protested strongly against a subsidy proposed for Mrs. Lloyd and against Mr. Edward Noel's defence of his son Frank. His pamphlet ended like this: 'Look up to Heaven, and in the ether a glow like unto a blushing star, warming and illuminating the earth that without it is ice-bound and murky, will strike upon your sense. The glow is the torch of the world, it is the reflection of Greece, it is the spirit of our planet, in a word, it is Greece! Fall on your knees, weep, repent, and you shall be worthy of forgiveness . . . Make haste! save yourselves, you and those who think with you, make haste! for otherwise you shall all run mad!' And even as late as 1904 a certain P. Giannopoulos could write: 'When Greece is silent, all humanity ceases. And when the Greek is silent, man is abolished. And when the Greek apes the barbarian, he commits suicide and a Greek is no longer upon earth. And Nature is no longer upon earth. Nor is Spirit. Nor is Beauty.' To the westerner, accustomed to judge by the single standard of factual truth, such sentiments could only appear to be the ramblings of delirium. Yet this Giannopoulos, we are assured, was a serious thinker, who greatly influenced such prominent persons as the political theorist Dragoumis and the poet Sikelianos.

It was easy to smile at a myth so sharply at variance with fact. Yet it might have been well to remember that this myth, so fondly cherished, had held the Greek people together as a race, and nerved it to endure in patience and hope nearly four centuries of slavery. And whether men smiled at it or not, they should at least have recognised it as a serious factor in the life of nineteenth-century Greece, and have taken it into consideration in framing their conduct towards her. But this double standard of consciousness, which anybody acquainted with Byzantine history would have understood at once, was outside the European experience.

It should, we say, have been clear to the English government that an incident so humiliating to the 'ethnic' pride as was the Dilessi affair would at once be reshaped on the 'ethnic' level of truth in such a manner as to absolve the 'ethnos' and its representatives from all responsibility in the occurrence. It was not only that individual Greeks were suspected, and more than suspected, of having had a hand in the affair. It was not only that the Greek prime minister himself was on record before the world as having stated his belief that prominent political figures had exploited, if not devised, the business for party purposes. It was also that foreign criticism had fixed on the whole of Greece without discrimination as the target for its abuse. The press of Europe, with a very few honourable exceptions, stigmatised the country as a nest of pirates, brigands and assassins. In farthest Germany, if Mr. Valaoritis was to be believed, men shut their doors against a Greek, and shunned him as they would have shunned a beast of prey. In face of this, it was not surprising that the 'ethnos' should have been quick to promulgate its own version of the affair, or should have resorted to any means in order to lend colour to it. By no possible intervention on the part of their own lawyers could the English compel the Greeks to disclose more than a fraction of the truth, or to acknowledge even that fraction. Any Greek witness of the educated class who told what everyone knew to be true would be regarded as one who had shamed the 'ethnos', and hence as a traitor and outcast. The humbler witnesses said merely what they had been told to say. Those who did at first, out of naïveté, tell what they believed to be truth were speedily induced upon re-examination to modify or withdraw their previous testimo-

ny, or even to deny that they had ever given it. Cookson and
Allan could do enough to exasperate Zaïmis and Limberákis, but
were quite unable to disinter a fragment of uncontroverted fact
from the shifting morass of evasion and perjury. To anyone
familiar with the Greek thought of the time, the verdict of such
an enquiry would have been a foregone conclusion: indeed, it
could have been written down without going to the trouble of
examining any witnesses at all. It was, that the whole guilt rest-
ed on foreign malefactors, aided by foreign – that is, Vlach –
peasants, and abetted by a foreigner, the Englishman Noel. That
the English government not only hoped for a different verdict,
but were even so certain of success that they were prepared to
put themselves in the wrong by insisting on the intervention of
English lawyers to achieve it, was the measure of their total
incomprehension of the people with whom they had to deal.

It is instructive to follow the stages by which the 'ethnic'
version of the affair crystallised into its final canonical shape. At
first, the Opposition had roundly accused General Soutzos,
who was notoriously a brigand-harbourer,[1] of criminal negli-
gence, if not of absolute complicity. Zaïmis, on his side, had
exposed to Mr. Erskine the part played in the affair by the
chiefs of the Opposition. The publication of his exposure in the
foreign press suddenly awakened the Greek public to their
country's discredit in the eyes of the outside world: and it
became overnight an article of truth that no political man of
any party had had the remotest contact with brigandage. 'What
honour,' cried Mr. Milisis, 'what respect can be enjoyed by a
nation whose chosen representatives are held up as such vile
and worthless creatures as to use brigands as tools of opposition?' Next, the brigands themselves had to be explained. At
first the ethnic champions, sailing on the old tack, found much
in them to condone and even to commend: they were the representatives of an old Hellenic tradition of noble outlawry and

[1] Wyse, 26.

liberty; they took to the hills in protest against injustice; they defended the weak, were generous to the poor, and slew only in self-defence. But very soon this line of reasoning was seen to be an anachronism. It was condemned as heretical: and the brigands were now denounced as wholly foreign cut-throats who battened on Greece with the connivance of Turkey. The next article in the canon went even further than the verdict of the judicial Enquiry. The conflicting testimonies of Alexander and Kamboutzis of their conversation at the well by Marathon were quietly forgotten: and the English themselves, out of mere bravado and in defiance of all warning and expostulation, were said to have ordered their coachmen to drive on at full gallop, leaving behind the soldiers who were to protect them and courting a disaster of whose probability they were fully apprised.[1] Lastly, having got themselves kidnapped, they were indebted for their murder to two of their own countrymen, Erskine and Noel. The 'ethnic' conscience had at last overcome all obstacles, and worked itself to rest.

The most potent influence in moulding the canonical Greek version of the Dilessi affair was a pamphlet written in English by an anonymous author, and published in London during the first days of June 1870. It was entitled *Notes on the recent Murders by Brigands in Greece.* The author was John Gennadios, a young Greek of distinguished parentage, at that time twenty-six years old and employed in the London office of Rhalli Brothers. He was a youth whose self-consequence was inversely proportionate to his inches; but it must be said at once that this self-consequence was not misplaced, since his intellectual endowments were much above the common. During three years of schooling at the Protestant College in Malta he had acquired a command of the English language which many Englishmen might have envied; and he wrote it with a style and facility nearly unexampled in a foreigner.[2] It is an odd circum-

[1] Milisis, *Two Speeches.*
[2] Rumbold, *Final Recollections,* 35.

stance that the pamphlet of Gennadios, considered merely on the linguistic level, is by far the ablest and most readable document of the many hundreds to which Dilessi gave rise. With this literary flair Gennadios combined a remarkable business acumen, and a talent for diplomacy which promised a brilliant career in the profession which he soon afterwards embraced.

Gennadios had been cut to the quick by the assaults launched on his nation by the English press and public. He treasured up the rhetorical gems scattered through the pages of the *Standard* and the *Pall Mall Gazette* with a painful scrupulosity amounting to masochism. At the end of six weeks he could endure it no longer. 'Our whole nation was vilified and dragged into the gutter; we were loaded with infamy, accused of all crimes, and made responsible for a murder committed by a band of malefactors; our past was cursed, our present imprecated, our future damned.' Despite the warning of his pusillanimous employers, that any published rejoinder would entail his dismissal from the firm, he sat down and in four nights of labour composed his *Notes*, which were privately printed and widely circulated in London.

Gennadios' pamphlet was in many ways a remarkable performance. Several points made in his defence of Greece were justified, and admirably set out. He had little difficulty in showing that the Greek ministers had not been antecedently aware of the intended excursion to Marathon and had therefore—*a fortiori*—given no guarantee of security to the excursionists. The measures taken by the government between 18 and 20 April, whether these were well or ill conceived, had been taken with the approval, if not at the suggestion, of the English minister Erskine: and this point was rightly made, not only by Gennadios, but by everybody else who was accurately informed of the circumstances.[1] Gennadios was again on the firmest ground in defending the decisions of the Zaïmis government to refuse

---

[1] Burnouf, 1001.

an amnesty, to reject the preposterous suggestion of a trial *in absentia*, and to protest against (for prevent it they could not) the intervention of Erskine and Cookson in the judicial process of the Enquiry. The inaccuracies and scurrility of the English newspapers he noted with proper contempt. Their allegations concerning the general state of public order in Greece were easy enough to refute, and easier still to retort. It was unnecessary to range as far afield as Hungary or Chile to find a condition of lawlessness fully as atrocious as any to be seen in Greece; and it could be said with absolute truth that it was far safer to take a stroll in the streets of Athens than in those of London.[1] 'And what', proceeded Gennadios, 'need we say of Ireland?' Alas, nothing; for the state of public order, or, to speak properly, of disorder, in County Meath and County Cavan would have disgraced the Cannibal Islands.

If Gennadios had been content to stick on these points, his pamphlet, besides being vigorous and sprightly, would also have been unexceptionable. But this was not his whole purpose. Greece must be shown to be absolutely blameless in every particular. And in two of the most material points the evidence – her own native evidence – was so strong against her that this could not be done without much omission, special pleading and prevarication. It is but fair to say that many of the most damning facts were not as yet public property, and many more were never to become so; but it was Gennadios' treatment of these two issues which led Lord Russell to exclaim in the House of Lords, 'I think a more lame defence of the Greek Government and a more total failure to make good the allegations of the writer, I have never known.'[2] The two points in question were of course the origin and purposes of the brigands, and the related, but far more delicate question of their clandestine connexions with political circles in Athens. Here

[1] Smith, 27.
[2] Official Report, II July, 1870.

no simple denial would suffice, and no simple *tu quoque*: no one ventured to accuse Mr. Disraeli of being in league with garroters, or Mr. Gladstone of maintaining gangs of Fenians and rapparees.

Gennadios saw plainly that the excuse of the 'noble kleft', which had been pleaded by his countryman Stephen Xenos as recently as 1865,[1] would no longer serve his turn. The Arvanitákis were degraded criminals, who must therefore be divested of any colour of Hellenism. The murders were done by 'brigands in Greece', not by 'Greek brigands'. This article was, we have seen, at once written into the canon; and the unfortunate Greek consul at Marseilles, who had thought himself to be on the party line in expounding the traditional origins of brigandage, was occasioned no small embarrassment by the *volte-face*. Now, it was true that only three of Takos' gang had been born actually within the borders of the Greek kingdom, although one of these three was the god-son of Mrs. Theagenis, and another, Yeroyiannis, was perhaps the most repulsive scoundrel of the whole twenty-one. Yet the remaining eighteen were all Greek-speaking and Orthodox Christians, who formed a part of exactly that persecuted population which Greece was claiming the right to free from Othoman oppression and annex to herself. The Arvanitákis brothers were, as we saw, very probably of that Greek family of nomad shepherds called Sarakatsans. Even had they been, as was now declared, Koutzo-Wallachians, yet if Greece had had to forgo all her citizens of that descent, she would have been the poorer by many eminent statesmen and many generous benefactors.[2] In short, if the Arvanitákis gang were not 'Greek' brigands, then they and their like were also not 'Greek' patriots, which they had been consistently held to be in the past. Gennadios unwittingly gave away his whole position when, early in his diatribe, he stated that, 'they [the brigands] looked hopefully to the coercion

[1] *East and West,* 104– 5.
[2] Finlay, VII, 197?.

which England and Italy would apply to their own country',[1] that is, to Greece: a revealing slip of the pen.

But it was over the question of the 'Alleged Complicity of Political Personages' that Gennadios was at his weakest and most disingenuous. The case for the defence was hopeless, and it is creditable at least to the courage of the author that he should have undertaken it. That brigandage had during thirty years been a regular political institution was a fact so notorious and so universally recognised in Greece that to attempt to disprove it was to argue that black was white. In common parlance brigandage and politics were almost interchangeable terms. In 1863 some English officers of the Corfu garrison, escorted, ominously enough, by Alexander Anemoyiannis, were held up and robbed on Pentelicus. One of the robbers turned out to be the son of the concierge of the English Legation. 'Ah, Your Excellency,' said the father to Mr. Scarlett, 'have I not always begged and entreated him to keep out of politics?' Pamphlets such as the capital *Reflexions on the establishment of order* by Colonel Koronaios, or the anonymous *Those responsible for brigandage in Peloponnesus*, might be not much read outside Greece. But the little book of Mr. Sotiropoulos had already been translated into English. Greek newspapers were daily referring to the contacts of their political opponents with brigands as to a matter of course.[2] English newspapers and periodicals were full of the reminiscences of recent travellers in Greece, all of whom had the same story to tell. Finally, the revelation made by Mr. Zaïmis to Erskine had been published, together with some very bitter reflexions, in *The Times* of 29 April.

That the brigands had contacts among the civil population was what not even Gennadios could deny. But he maintained that these were persons of like standing with themselves. He

[1] *Notes,* 24.
[2] e.g. *Aión*, 18 April 21; *Palingenesia*, 18 April; *Mellon*, 15 April; and some frank articles of *La Grèce*, a French-language newspaper of high quality, 21, 28 May and 4 June 1870.

ignored the glaring improbability that Takos and Christos, on no better assurance than that of some Athenian riff-raff, would have turned down £25,000 and stood to the death by their conviction that an amnesty could and would be given. Over the disclosure of Mr. Zaïmis, his only resource was to abuse the plaintiff's attorney: Mr. Erskine was to blame for the whole misunderstanding; yet, instead of admitting his error like a man, Erskine had made some hair-splitting distinctions between 'leading members' and the 'leader' of the Opposition! Zaïmis, with his 'honest but suspicious disposition', had doubtless implied that persons had been active in a spirit of opposition to his government, but assuredly he had never meant to implicate Greek political circles. Who then were these sinister advisers who had egged on Takos to press his demands? They were – the Vlach Costa Seliamis; and George Yannou Arvanitákis, the servant of the Englishman Frank Noel!

Gennadios of course could not be aware that Seliamis had been acting on the instructions of General Soutzos, or that Zaïmis had in private confessed the accuracy of Erskine's report. But, in aspersing Frank Noel he not only gave a very sinister impetus to those who were conducting the official Enquiry, but was also, in his 'ethnic' enthusiasm, betraying a friendship of long standing. He had been intimate with, and had received much kindness from, Edward Noel and his children, Frank and Alice. Frank, he now declared, had been hoodwinked by Takos throughout the proceedings: for Takos, despite Frank's express statement, had in fact never had the smallest intention of accepting the Greek government's terms. But far worse than this: Frank had – unwittingly perhaps – been directly responsible for Takos' obstinacy. The unlucky postscript in Herbert's letter to Erskine of 20 April made it clear that Frank thought 'that all the demands of the brigands ought to be complied with'. Doubtless his opinion had been known to his servant, George Yannou, the brother of Takos: and Gennadios had

it for a fact that George had been a principal influence in persuading his brothers to stick out for the amnesty. The case was
plain.

Gennadios seems not to have realised that in making these
baseless and unjustifiable innuendoes he was mortally wound-
ing his friends, or that he was casting on Frank the suspicion of
a crime 'scarcely within the bounds of human wickedness'. The
sneering tone of his references to Noel added insult to the
injury. His only excuse must be that he regarded the claims of
the 'ethnos' as overriding the decencies of private conduct.
'The baseness of this insinuation', wrote Edward Noel, '. . . is
only equalled by insinuations equally vile which appeared in a
pamphlet in this country, written by a Greek who had received
numerous proofs of kindness from myself and my family, and
who, I suppose, considered ingratitude and slander a patriotic
duty . . . It is to be hoped for the honour of humanity in general and of the Greek nation in particular, that there are not
many such of the "race of Zeus".'[1]

Frank Noel was not the only innocent foreigner whom
Gennadios saw fit to press into the service of ethnic exoneration. In *The Times* of 18 May had appeared a letter signed 'G.'
which impugned the honour of Lord Muncaster in not returning to captivity after his release on 13 April. In his Notes Gennadios returned to the attack on Muncaster, accused him by
implication of false testimony, and attributed to his failure to
return to captivity a portion of the responsibility for the dread-
ful fate of his friends. The imputation was beneath contempt.
Muncaster, who had secured the whole ransom within twelve
hours of his return to Athens, had been under no obligation
whatsoever to return to Keramidi or Oropós; and in doing so
he would merely have added to the anxiety and dismay of his
friends.

[1] Noel, *Letters*, 17. The 'race of Zeus', or 'Dios Genna', was the pseudonym of
Gennadios.

Such then were the guiding lines for the Enquiry, devised in the fertile brain of John Gennadios. Six months later the official findings confirmed those of Gennadios to the letter: for the only persons against whom a bill was found were some shepherds, Seliamis, George Yannou and Frank Noel. Whatever we may think of his candour, we cannot deny that Gennadios had rendered an important service to the discovery of 'ethnic' truth. And shortly afterwards his country received him into her diplomatic service, where he rose with the rapidity which his talents so clearly merited. He seems to have believed that even his breach with the Noels might be healed, and in December he presented himself at Edward Noel's house in Hampstead. But he was not received. 'I am delighted', wrote Finlay, 'at the dismissal of the impudent elf Gennadios.'[1]

[1] Finlay to Edward Noel, 31 December 1870 (N.-B.).

# CHAPTER SEVEN

# THE ENQUIRY

'The various stages of it [the Enquiry] that have been gone
through have tended to open up more and more what is painful
and what is shameful in the present condition of Greece.'

MR. GLADSTONE

Meantime in Athens and over the countryside the justices were
busy pursuing enquiries and taking depositions. The investigation reached far and wide, but it was not the more fruitful on
that account. Very few of those examined corroborated one
another's testimony. Large numbers of witnesses came forward
to volunteer important information, which they afterwards
modified, reversed, or altogether withdrew. Many saw in the
Enquiry a golden opportunity to pay off old scores by violating the Ninth Commandment, and of this process Frank Noel,
though the best known, was by no means the only victim. A
farrago of completely false testimony was compiled by the
'notorious Juge de Paix Papayannou',[1] which led Cookson
during several weeks on an absurd wild-goose chase.

A very short time sufficed to persuade Mr. Cookson of the
formidable nature of his task. It was not that there was too little evidence: there was far too much, and almost none of it was
to be relied upon. 'It happens every day and every hour,' he told
Erskine 'that the most substantial looking fabric of testimony,
on being touched by the spear of cross-examination or
enquiry, vanishes into the flimsiest atmosphere of doubt and
suspicion.' Moreover, the press and public in Athens followed

[1] Papafrangos to Kondostavlos, 14 December 1870.

131

Cookson's own proceedings with extreme dislike and jealousy. Early in July the prosecutor Limberákis told Zaïmis that he was so much harassed by the interference of Cookson and Allan that he could endure it no longer, and he threatened to 'throw upon some other person his unpalatable duty, if any person could be found to perform it.'[1]

Of the movements of the brigand gang before their *coup* near Marathon, a comparatively clear picture did at last emerge. They had originally numbered twenty-eight. They had crossed into Greece from Turkey towards the end of January, and had skirmished with the gendarmerie in the province of Levadeia, with a loss to themselves of one man. They had pushed eastwards into the province of Thebes, and on 2 February had again been attacked, this time with the loss of six men. After a sojourn near Rhitsona, where they had been entertained by a gossip ('koumbáros') of the Arvanitákis, one Elias Kolovós, they had turned southwards into the Megarid, which they entered on 12 February. During the next six weeks they had remained in that province; moving about from one *liméri* to another in the hills round Villia, and being supplied by friendly shepherds. The next piece of firm evidence dated from the night of 27–28 March, the night before the municipal elections. According to the deposition of the shepherd Loukos, who later of course withdrew it, the band had on that night advanced to within half an hour's distance of the town of Villia, and sent for the mayor of the place, Mr. George Maléas. This Maléas and his brother Dimitrios, parliamentary deputy for the Megarid, were the local political 'bosses', who ran the district in the interest and under the protection of the faction of Mr. Koumoundouros. This interview with Mr. Maléas, and his subsequent return as mayor of the town,[2] seem to have concluded the Megarian commitments of the gang, which now went east-

[1] Erskine to Hammond, 5 July 1870.
[2] Erskine to Clarendon, 23 June 1870.

wards into Attica, which they entered by way of Chassiá. They crossed the Attic plain by night, passing near Ano Liossia, and on or about 3 April established themselves in Mount Pentelicus, where they received food and shelter from the prior and steward of the Pendéli monastery. These two persons, Parthenios Vretas and Hadji-Loundzis, men of the vilest character, were afterwards acquitted of harbouring by the official Enquiry; but the charge was found to be proved when in the following year they were taken up for the murder by poison of a servant who had threatened to inform against them.[1]

Near the monastery the gang remained until 7 April, the day on which the Muncasters and Vyner had arrived in Athens. They then shifted to *liméria* nearer the high road to Marathon, and close to the sheep-folds of some pastoral families named Megayannis and Kapouralos, with whom they were familiar. Here, it was said, on 8 April they had nearly captured some American excursionists to the battlefield. What information they received from Athens during the next four days, apart from such as could be got by sending Megayannis thither to buy them shoes, was never divulged. What did emerge was that during all or part of these four days the chiefs had been absent from the band. The responsibility for persuading Takos to stay near the place of the abduction until 11 April was laid at the door of a peasant called Goggos by one of the captive brigands; who afterwards—need it be said?—withdrew his evidence. But none of the captured brigands would say where their chiefs had been during the vital period, and in all probability none of them knew: since Takos and Christos, with their cousins Stathakis and Patsiouras, formed an inner executive committee, which kept their plans very much to themselves.

The next question of importance to discover was whether the capture of Lord Muncaster's party had been planned or was fortuitous: and here the evidence, most of which was ignored

[1] Stuart to Granville, 11 August 1871.

by the report of the Enquiry, appeared strongly in favour of the former. Lord Muncaster himself, who was examined in Athens on 26 April, deposed: 'My impression is that they [the brigands] knew who we were before our capture, because on the day after our capture, in a conversation which our courier had with the brigands, he said, on turning towards me, "they know who you are, and what you are worth".' Frank Noel, examined on 25 April at Chalkis, was yet more explicit: 'They [the brigands] said in my presence, "they gave us the Englishmen", but they did not specify who; and Mr. Herbert told me that very often the brigand chief Tako Arvanites told him that they had captured them through treachery.' Alexander Anemoyannis, the dragoman, had been most positive of all: he told the captives that the brigands had told him 'that their passing on the day of their capture, and their excursion to Marathon, had been communicated to them from Athens, by persons holding high positions.' On the other side, much was made of Muncaster's statement that the brigands, on learning of the identity and importance of their captives, began singing and dancing for joy: which, it was said, was proof that they had had no previous knowledge of those with whom they had to deal. Proof, however, is too strong a word. Demonstrations of joy may well have been indulged in by the subaltern members of the crew: it was not recorded that Takos and Christos danced or sang.

That some prominent political person or persons had exploited, as distinct from devising, the capture, scarcely admitted of any doubt at all. Here the disclosure made by Mr. Zaïmis to Erskine on 15 April was of great weight: the very fact that the prime minister should have stated and believed such a thing to be probable, in a society such as that of Athens, where owing to the national pastime of spying on one's neighbour even the most secret transactions were generally notorious, strongly suggested that his suspicions were but too well founded. It was a fact that on the night of Thursday, 14 April, two emissaries other than those dispatched by government had visited the brigands with a letter or letters from Athens. It was a fact that from that moment the chiefs had stood by their conviction that their demands must be granted, with a tenacity which even the assurances of Mr. Noel had with difficulty shaken and no one else had been able to shake at all. It was a fact that Herbert had stated that Takos' actions were guided by his correspondents in Athens. Were there not therefore the strongest reasons for believing that his confidence and conviction were engendered by some authority, some 'strong-minded person' (as Takos put it), of an importance at least equal to that of Mr. Zaïmis?

With all this in mind, we are compelled to look very closely at a confidential dispatch of Mr. Erskine, dated 7 May, which may suggest that quite early on in the Enquiry Erskine had for a moment the key to the whole mystery in his hands, and then, in his blundering fashion, allowed it to slip from his fingers. One of the first persons to be taken up and examined, after the captured brigands themselves, was of course Costa Seliamis, the go-between who, on the orders of General Soutzos, had thrice visited the band. Seliamis was first examined by the Chief of Police, who passed the substance of his deposition to Mr. Erskine.

He [Seliamis] is reported [wrote Erskine] to have said that on one occasion he came up to town the bearer of nine letters – viz. one for General Soutzos, one for Mr. Zaïmis, one for me from Mr. Herbert, one for the Italian Minister from Count de Boÿl one for Lord Muncaster from Mr.Vyner, one from Mr. Lloyd to his wife, *one for M. Coumoundouros (I conclude, from the brigands),*[1] one for an officer who is now at Nauplia, and whose connection with the brigands is about to be enquired into; and one to a person named Nasi – but I have marked this despatch confidential because the statement as to M. Coumoundouros still rests on hearsay and it would be a serious matter publicly to implicate the Head of the Opposition on such evidence. I closely questioned the Director of Police as to these statements and he is quite positive on the subject . . .[2]

[1] Our italics.
[2] Erskine to Clarendon, 7 May 1870.

At his re-examination on 10 May, at which Erskine was present, Seliamis withdrew nearly the whole of this testimony. At first he denied all knowledge of any letters whatever. Then he admitted that perhaps after all there had been some letters, but he had not been the bearer. How many letters had there been? Three or four, perhaps: he couldn't exactly remember. Nine? Oh, no: he had never spoken of nine! And so on. Erskine threw up his hands in disgust, remarking, 'nothing that he could say ought to be received as evidence except against himself.'[1]

But Mr. Erskine was probably too hasty. The fact that Seliamis, after an interval, withdrew his initial statement, does not prove that statement to have been false, either in whole or in part. It appears, on the contrary, to have been reasonable and consistent. Had there been no such letters, or had he not been the carrier of them, it is scarcely credible that Selamis should have been able to invent, with complete accuracy, the senders and recipients of at least four of them. Now, letters from Herbert, Boÿl, Lloyd and Vyner, addressed respectively to Erskine, Minerva, Mrs. Lloyd and Muncaster, are in fact extant, all dated Saturday, 16 April. On this day Seliamis did in fact visit the brigands for the last time; and that he should have carried these and other letters back to Athens is probable enough. Letters from Takos to Soutzos and Zaïmis of the same date are easily explicable: they would have contained a firm rejection of the government's terms and a demand for more reputable envoys. The ninth recipient, whose name was given by Seliamis as Nasi, was none other than Nasi or Naso Ioannou, the government emissary who had on the previous Thursday embezzled Takos' £30 and not reappeared. It is certain that Takos would have had a message for him. It should be noted that much of what Seliamis said about his previous mission on 14 April to Keramidi was demonstrably true, and was accepted as such by

[1] Erskine to Clarendon, 12 May 1870.

Captain Moschovakis.[1] All in all, we cannot exclude the possibility that what he said about the nine letters was also true. And if so, why then—! But the point was dropped, and not alluded to again by Erskine, or Clarendon, or anybody else.

Evidence from the six captured brigands was taken at several examinations in the Mendresé gaol, part of it in the presence of Erskine or Cookson. But nothing of what they had to tell was acceptable without independent confirmation. The prisoners were herded together in a single chamber, together with twenty or thirty other malefactors or suspects. Anyone who wished might obtain access to them from outside, if he chose to wait until an officer belonging to his political faction came on guard and admitted him. The testimony, taken at three separate interrogations, of Periklis Lioris, the most communicative of the brigands, was a tangle of truth and falsehood, and neither Cookson nor Erskine could say where the one ended and the other began. Lioris had begun by denouncing the brothers Maléas of Villia, where he was himself native. He then turned to another area, the island of Euboea, with its capital Chalkis. He said that when Takos was in flight after the clash in which Christos and the captives had been slain, those with him roundly cursed his folly in rejecting ransom and safe-conduct and insisting on amnesty. Takos had replied, with tears, that it was not he who was to blame, but those 'Great Ones', who had written from Chalkis persuading him to stick fast. Pressed further, Lioris stated that among those who had so written were a Mr. Thanopoulos, an official in the Department of Justice at Athens, and Mr. Basil Boudouris, an ex-deputy and landed proprietor of Euboea. These statements well illustrated the difficulty of Cookson's position: for it was virtually certain that Thanopoulos had had no hand in the affair; whereas it was far from certain that Boudouris, whose connexions with brigandage were well known in his island, was equally blameless.

[1] See *Official Report of the Trial*, proceedings of 10 May 1871.

Four members of the Greek cabinet—Zaïmis, Delyannis, Avyerinós and Sarávas—were most eager to conclude the Enquiry with the minimum of delay. But here they encountered opposition, not only from Erskine, but also from their three colleagues, Valaoritis, Tombazis and the new war minister, General Smolensk. The first step was to dispose of the captured brigands, most of whom would, or more probably could, tell nothing of importance. Their trial was fixed for 21 May, in the Varvakeion. Cookson and Allan, very inadvisedly, occupied seats immediately behind the presiding judges. The prisoners were brought in, most of them wounded and two of them half dead with gangrene. Some formal evidence was given by witnesses, who included Colonel Theagenis—'a small, pedantic officer, declaiming with his hands in a forced, theatrical manner, as though he had been the hero of some glorious victory.'[1] Neither he nor anyone else was pressed in regard to the details of this glorious victory: and here perhaps we may detect in the proceedings a certain official reticence.[2] The case against the accused was plain enough. They had asked for two Athenian lawyers of their choice, Goulimis and Kolokotronis, to defend them; but these advocates could do little in their speeches but deplore the sad state of their country and the injustice of the foreign newspapers in maligning her. The death sentence was passed on all six prisoners and, a month later, carried out on five of them by public guillotining in the Champ de Mars. The prisoner Lioris, who seemed likely to furnish more material information, was at Erskine's suggestion respited.

But such evidence as these wretches had to give formed but a small part of what had to be taken. The most active

[1] *Pall Mall Gazette*, 1 July 1870.
[2] Finlay to Edward Noel, 9 November 1870 (N.-B.): 'it [the Greek government] meddled in the trial of the brigands to keep away the evidence of the officers who were present at the engagement, in order to save the reputation of Theagenis and Erskine.'

enquiries during May were directed towards discovering the brigands' connexions in the Megarid. It was delicate ground to explore, since the brothers Maléas were powerful and well protected; but the evidence against them was in sum so incontrovertible that they were in early June actually arrested and held for a time in prison, the only persons of their class to be so detained throughout the Enquiry. It was not suggested that they had had any hand in the Dilessi murders, but that they had harboured and exploited the Arvanitákis for political purposes. The Koumoundouros faction was in a fury: it believed, rightly enough, that if the brothers Maléas had been adherents of Mr. Zaïmis, they would not have been subjected to this indignity; and it cast about desperately, but without success, for evidence of equal weight which should touch Mr. Dimitrios Averoff, the chief supporter of Mr. Zaïmis in Euboea. These partisans need not have troubled themselves. The government was rapidly disintegrating, and Mr. Zaïmis himself was being shepherded by the Russian minister Novikow into the fold of the russophil Koumoundouros. The Maléas were perfectly safe: and two applications by Mr. Erskine that the mayor of Villia should be suspended from his office were dismissed by Mr. Zaïmis.

It was however in the course of the Megarian enquiry that Cookson obtained his first direct insight into the methods by which the rural areas of Greece were organised and governed, concerning which he seems to have had no previous knowledge. His description of this revelation was most illuminating:

As an interesting illustration [he wrote to Erskine on 16 June] of what is more or less the general condition of many districts of Greece, I may draw your attention to the evidence of the three inhabitants of Vilia . . . From the narrative of these three men − a Notary or Law-Agent of the lowest class − a tavern keeper and a shepherd − it was not difficult to draw the picture of the way in which local politicians of the class of the Brothers Malléa employ the predominating influences which they enjoy from their wealth, their family tenure of every municipal office, and their terrorism by the agency of brigands, for the oppression of the poorer villagers and peasantry. The evident terror with which these men and other witnesses spoke even to one another of facts which must have been known to every woman in the village will have reminded you of the secret tribunals of Venice. This apprehension probably solves the mystery why when a fact is so universally known as the political nature of brigandage it is so difficult to prove the complicity of particular persons. In every centre of brigandage its local patron would appear to have some agent who has family or other connections with his particular band—through whom he deals with them and through whom the brigands, whose usual haunt is on the hills, communicate generally by night with their patron.

The agent in this instance was the family of Periklis Lioris. Cookson added that, such was the savage vengeance meted out by both brigand and patron, no peasant would willingly so much as be in possession of facts which might be 'dangerous to him'.[1]

Such was the state of intimidation and corruption which the evidence, hesitant and evasive as it might be, gradually exposed to the eyes of the astonished Cookson. It was not to be supposed that any Greek government would tamely permit this evidence to become international property without making every effort to smother it. The first step in this direction was discernible in the middle of June. Zaïmis, already contemplating a *rapprochement* with Mr. Koumoundouros, then made a resolute effort to bring the Enquiry itself to an abrupt termination. This provoked an immediate and open rupture in his cabinet. Mr. Valaoritis told Erskine that he had repeatedly observed his prime minister stifling evidence which tended towards inculpating his supporters in Euboea. This was probably untrue, since no evidence subsequently came to light which connected any of the Averoffs with the gang or their activities. But at least Valaoritis believed that Zaïmis was untrustworthy; and at last

[1] Cookson to Erskine, 16 June 1870; Erskine to Clarendon, 23 June 1870.

he and his two supporters, Tombazis and Smolensk, began to act as a nearly independent administration within the government itself.

A second step by which Greek responsibility might be disguised was by shifting it, should this be possible, on to the shoulders of a foreigner, the unhappy Mr. Frank Noel.[1] This young gentleman, who suffered by the affair more undeservedly than any except the victims themselves, was now in his twenty-sixth year. He had during three years been the proprietor of the large and fertile estate of Achmetaga in Euboea, from which his father, Edward Noel had retired to England in 1867.

Edward Noel was a cousin of Anne Isabella, Lady Byron, the poet's widow. She had commissioned her cousin in 1831 to visit Greece, in order to collect information at first hand about her husband's last days and death at Missolonghi. On his way back in 1832 Edward Noel visited Euboea. The boundaries of the new kingdom of Greece had recently been drawn, and Euboea fell within them. The Turkish proprietors were therefore eager to dispose of their estates to the first bidders, and Noel, in association with a Swiss named Müller, sank his small capital in the purchase of the Achmetaga property. On it he settled down, and began, with very little idea of the difficulties to be encountered, to farm his lands and to care for his tenantry according to the most enlightened principles of the west. However, he soon had reason to doubt the wisdom of his choice. His Byronic affinities did him no service in the country of his adoption. As a foreigner he was disliked, and as a prospering foreigner he was envied, by his neighbours. He was subjected to a continual series of petty tyrannies, culminating, on 26 March 1855, in the sacking of Achmetaga by a brigand gang whose arrival was certainly not unprompted. During four hours the house was looted and its inhabitants terrorised.

[1] Noel, *Letters,* 8.

Noel's elder daughter, aged sixteen, died of shock a few weeks later. His son Frank, then a child of ten years old, remembered to his dying day how the brigands had danced on the drawing-room table, and had peered with curiosity and astonishment into the looking-glasses that hung on the walls.[1] After such an outrage, which King Otho's government had not lifted a finger to redress,it was not very probable that any of the Noel family should have felt any sympathy for the institution of brigandage.

Edward Noel, as we have said, retired to Hampstead in 1867, leaving Frank to manage the estate. The son was an honest and courageous young fellow, whose only faults were such as age seldom fails to correct: an excess of self-confidence, a choleric disposition, and a tactlessness arising from inability to keep his temper under prudent control. He had formed a close friendship with the brothers Dimitrios and Avyerinós Averoff, and with Avyerinós' son Michael, a parliamentary deputy and his own near contemporary. During the parliamentary election of 1869 he had, although a foreigner, shown zeal in canvassing for the Averoff interest, and had thus aroused, or confirmed, the hostility of three powerful neighbours in the island, Messrs. Boudouris, Kriezotis and Tombazis. Boudouris had summoned a gang of brigands into the island for the purpose of 'influencing' the voters. They were fêted at Limni, where they dined with the mayor; and, at the instigation of Boudouris, they sent a threatening letter to Noel. Noel exposed this manoeuvre to George Finlay, and applied for protection to Mr. Erskine. Finlay sent Noel's letter under private cover to the editor of *The Times*; but the result of the election was such that Mr. Erskine believed that Noel would now be adequately protected from annoyance, and saw no need to intervene.[2]

[1] Information of his son-in-law, Mr. Philip Noel-Baker. The letters of Edward Noel to George Finlay, which described the Outrage, were shown to Nassau Senior, who published long extracts from them: Senior, 340–6.
[2] Finlay to Mowbray Morris, 6 June 1869; Erskine to Finlay, 10 June 1869 (AG 1869).

Frank Noel was much blamed by his family in England for mixing himself up in Greek politics. Finlay however was of a different opinion. He pointed out that to live on an estate in Greece, isolated from the political interest and protection of a strong party, was to ask for trouble; and that the only circumstance which since 1867 had protected Frank from a repetition, or repetitions, of the outrage of 1855 was his known connexion with the Averoffs, that is to say, with the Zaïmis-Delyannis faction. However that might be, Noel had played the full part of a Greek landowner, not only in his political but also in his social affiliations. His circle of 'gossipred' was perforce a wide one; and within his circle came two Vlachs, or shepherds, named Nikolaos and Apostolis. Frank was godfather to the son of Nikolaos, and had stood as groomsman at the marriage of Apostolis. These two shepherds had been, and still were, in his service, because he had found them honest and industrious. But to have employed them was, as it turned out, unfortunate: for their surname was Arvanitákis. They were the brothers of the brigand chiefs Takos and Christos, as well as of George Yannou and the cattle-dealing Dinos.[1]

This unlucky connexion, in origin perfectly innocent, gave rise after the Dilessi affair to much prejudice and misunderstanding in England, where only the vaguest notions about Greek rural life were entertained. It was true that by assuming the relationship of 'koumbáros' (compère or gossip) with two of the Arvanitákis brothers, Noel was, by the custom of the country, the patron and protector of them all. They had become his 'men', in the sense that they were bound to him as clients.

[1] Frank Noel to Alice Noel, 6 July 1870: 'I really, my dear Alice, am not responsible for any "vague" notions that people in England may have upon the affairs of Greece ... One day the wife of the said Koleos [Nikolaos] passed through the village with a very fat baby in her arms. I was asked to stand god-father to it, and accordingly did so ... Time passed on ... when one fine day I received a note from Daphnonda, inviting me to be Nonôs [sponsor] at the marriage of Apostolis Arvanitákis. As I had never seen a Vlach wedding, and as I thought it was not advisable under the circumstance to refuse, I accepted ...' *Letters*, 58.

When therefore he referred (as he did) to George Yannou as his 'man', most people in England naturally assumed that George was his employee or paid servant; but this he very emphatically and, we do not doubt, very sincerely denied. And to assume from this spiritual relationship, one which bound every peasant in the land to one local landowner or other, that Noel must of necessity have regarded the interests of Takos and Christos as paramount, even to the exclusion of those of his friends Herbert and Lloyd and of his countryman Vyner, was merely farcical. Yet this was in fact the prejudice against him, not only in Greek and in some English circles, but even in the English Legation itself.

There is reason to think that Erskine's personal hostility to Frank Noel was of several months', if not of years', growth. Noel's bearing towards the minister, a man of more than twice his age and very much more than twice his importance, had from the first been lacking in proper deference. His requests took the form of demands, and peremptory demands at that. Whatever difficulties his schemes encountered he expected Erskine to override. He seemed to believe that the English minister was set in Athens for the primary purpose of maintaining the importance of English residents in Greece, and to expect him to act in as high-handed a fashion as Lord Stratford had for decades acted at Constantinople. The Dilessi tragedy set the match to a large amount of combustible material. Noel had been justifiably incensed by the ineptitude shown by both Erskine and Theagenis in that affair.

> I must own [he wrote] that it is impossible to forgive the part Mr. Erskine has taken in this horrible affair of Oropós,[1] though I feel convinced that he acted to the best of his judgment; but it seems that his judgment was not over clear during that sad time. He surely acted very weakly in taking part in the private councils of the Government, who now of course try to put all the blame on him, saying that nothing was done without the consent of Mr. Erskine.

[1] Noel, *Letters*, 30. 'Too true', commented Finlay in the margin of his copy.

Noel, no doubt, had a perfect right to this opinion, which was fully endorsed by Finlay. But he had not the common sense to keep it to himself. He published it widely among any, whether English or Greeks, who cared to listen. If he had had any idea of the patience and cunning with which successive Greek webs were to be woven about him, he would have done his utmost, whatever he might think in private, to keep on the right side of Erskine, who was the only person in Greece in a position to help him. As it was, when the blow fell, he found Mr. Erskine very little disposed to strain his authority in defence of one by whom he had been so mercilessly assailed.

An apparently reasonable presumption that Noel, out of his spiritual relationship to Nikolaos and Apostolis Arvanitákis, should have interested himself on behalf of their scoundrel brothers also, was not the only, or the most important, piece of evidence which seemed to tell against him. On the dead body of Christos Arvanitákis, had been found several documents, among which was one recovered by Colonel Theagenis and sent by him to Mr. Zaïmis. There could be no doubt that this document was an authentic communication sent to the brigands before the murders: the only questions were, what did it mean and who had sent it? The letter purported to run as follows:

CHALKIS, 18 April 1870

Brothers! We are well, and hope you are too. What you have done about the captives is well. As our friends inform us, you should not ask for money, but insist as much as you can on the amnesty. All our friends are sure this will be given. When they [?I] have settled matters in a certain place [? on a certain day], they [?I ? we] will come to you on foot [?I will come if I can]. If they [? I] don't take care to send somebody else to our 'koumbáros'. We have a commission (parangelía) that you must by all means receive. I saw our 'koumbáros' today, who sends you many respectful salutations (proskynímata). And I am your brother.

GEORGE YANNOU.

P.S.-Stick fast to the amnesty as much as you can!
To Dimitrios and Christos, wherever they are.

On the publication of a version of this text, certain conclusions were leapt at instantly. George Yannou, the signatory,
was the brother of the Arvanitákis chiefs, and with him Noel
had gone to Oropós from Chalkis on 19 April. Noel himself
was the 'koumbáros', since, as gossip of Nikolaos and Apostolis,
he might by extension be considered 'koumbáros' of Takos,
Christos and George also. Did it not therefore follow that it
was Noel who had been the principal in persuading Takos to
stand firm in his resistance to the offers of Colonel Theagenis?
That, in short, it was he who, without regard to the wretched
captives, had gone to Oropós with the single purpose of
exhorting his 'men' to reject the reasonable terms of the Greek
government?

A moment's reflection would suffice to convince the candid reader that these conclusions were illogical. Even if George
Yannou had been the author of the letter (though, to be sure,
he was illiterate), and even if Frank Noel had been the 'koumbáros' in question (though, in the plethora of possible alternatives, this was far from certain), even so it should have been
obvious that a clear distinction was drawn in the text between
the 'koumbáros' and the 'friends'. The former was merely stated to be in need of an emissary or escort. It was the latter
whose advice was strong for insistence upon the amnesty. But
in fact the use of the word 'proskynímata', 'respectful greetings'
or 'salaams', was against the identification of Noel with the
'koumbáros': since this was a word used by a social inferior to
a social superior, and Noel was certainly not the inferior of the
Arvanitákis. Moreover, a literal or holograph version of the text
was not published: only versions of it that had been corrected
according to the 'taste and fancy' of the editors. The original
purport was in several passages highly dubious. It is unnecessary to perplex the reader with the minutiae of Greek dialects
and orthography: suffice to it say that in certain dialects, including the Sarakatsan, the vowel 'o' was pronounced, and could be

written, as 'ou', and the final 'n', which forms a valuable deter-
minative of person and number, could be omitted. Thus, for
example, if the original version read 'tha erthou' (as it did), this
might be either 'I will come' or 'they will come', or, if the two
following letters were 'me', 'we will come'. It was, in such circumstances, not difficult for Noel's counsel to poke any number of holes in the official reading of this controversial and
partly illegible document.

The machinations against Noel began very early, but it was
some months before he became the chief target of the government Enquiry. The reason for this was that while Mr. Zaïmis
remained in office, Noel was partly shielded by his connexion
with the Averoff family. The first plot against him, which was
laid during May and June, was the invention of his local political enemies, Messrs. Boudouris, Tombazis and Kriezotis, and
was directed against the Averoffs even more than against himself. It was the silliest affair; yet not without an element of danger, since Emmanuel Tombazis had the ear of his brother
George, the minister of marine, and George was the trusted ally
of Mr. Valaoritis. Mr. Erskine, for his part, put all his faith in
Valaoritis.

The aim of the plot was to show that after the Dilessi affair
Takos and the remnant of his gang had crossed over into
Euboea, and had taken shelter on the properties of Noel and
the Averoffs, by whom they were even now being succoured
and concealed. That there was not a vestige of truth in the alle-
gation was a minor difficulty, very easily overcome. A few art-
ful ingredients were dropped into the simmering cauldron of
tittle-tattle at Chalkis, and the whole brew came boiling over.
Noel was behaving 'curiously'. He had been threatened with
arrest by the public prosecutor. He had let fall information
about Takos which he could have known only from close
acquaintance with the recent movements of the gang. 'Evidence' was next concocted with the help of two wretches

named Daras, who lived at St. Anna. What inducements were offered to them to tell circumstantial stories which they knew to be false, is unknown. But in the case of a certain Sarandaris, Noel believed that the inducements had been of a very practical description. This man, said Noel, who was an employee of Mr. James Tombazis, had been summoned to his master's house, and there, in the presence of a juge de paix called Papanastasiou, had been put to the torture to induce him to bear false witness.[1] When he refused, his deposition was forged. This frightful story rests on Noel's statement, and the reader must be left to determine the degree of its probability.

Emmanuel Tombazis, through his brother and Valaoritis, next opened a correspondence with Mr. Erskine; and in the middle of June one of the Daras was sent to Athens to tell his story to the English minister. Erskine lent a willing ear to anything which reflected unfavourably on Noel, especially when it was backed by the opinion of Valaoritis. He swallowed the whole fabrication, bait and hook. He wrote to Lord Clarendon on 18 June that Tombazis' agent Daras considered 'even Mr. Noel's conduct as most suspicious'. This dispatch, which reached London after Clarendon's death, was sent to Lord de Grey, the Lord President. 'I don't believe a word of this', he minuted; 'it is evidently the desire of the Greek government to ruin Mr. Noel. I trust they will not be allowed to do so.'

The deluded Erskine readily fell in with the plan of the equally deluded Valaoritis, who, in his general distrust of all landed proprietors, made no distinction of persons, to send a secret military expedition into Euboea in order to round up Takos; and he went so far in his folly as to lend the services of an English naval vessel, H.M.S. *Jaseur*, to transport the Greek troops thither. The *battue* of course was a complete fiasco: since Takos and his men were not on the island, and never had been. The soldiers marched in, and after a few days of good living at

[1] Noel to Erskine, 5 October 1870; Cookson to Noel, 18 October 1870.

free quarters, marched out again. In vain did Noel protest that 'the whole thing is a farce of the most vile and abominable nature, and got up to implicate me.' Even after the failure of the expedition, Erskine stubbornly refused to be convinced. Emmanuel Tombazis continued to urge that the Averoffs were guilty and were using Noel as their cat's-paw, 'so that little by little they have entangled him, and now he finds himself in a kind of drunken state, so that if you do not arrive at any satisfactory results the Inquiry must be recommenced'.[1] Takos had been fed by three of Averoff's and Noel's men in the sheepfolds of Daras; and if he had not been found, why, then one of the members of the Zaïmis government must have warned him to make himself scarce!

Not until 30 September could Mr. Erskine bring himself to admit, on the plain evidence of the nomarch of Attica, Mr. Antoniadis, that 'it was quite impossible that Takos could have been in Euboea since the massacre at Dilessi, and that the statement to this effect was concocted by the brothers Dara in order to injure Messrs. Averoff and Noel'.[2] Of all the blunders of Erskine this was the most shameful and ridiculous. 'It is sad', wrote Finlay, 'to think that a man so weak in judgment and so rash in statement should be the person who guided, or misguided, the British Government in its researches during the enquiry.'[3]

This ludicrous exploit administered the final blow to the divided cabinet of Mr. Zaïmis. Valaoritis had so profoundly mistrusted his chief that he had concerted the expedition to Euboea without even informing the prime minister of what he was doing. This seems hardly credible; but that the English minister should have lent his support appeared, if possible, more

---

[1] Emmanuel Tombazis to George Tombazis, 22 July 1870.
[2] Erskine to Granville, 30 September 1870; cf. 24 August 1870.
[3] Finlay to Edward Noel (draft), 24 March 1871 (AG 1871): see also Erskine to Clarendon, 18 June; Emm. Tombazis to Erskine, 13 June; Cdr. Hotham to Erskine, 10 July; Noel to Erskine, 18 July 1870; and Noel, *Letters*, 62, 78– 9.

astonishing still. The fiasco showed that the government's days were numbered. Mr. Erskine hoped for a moment that Mr. Valaoritis himself might be induced to form a ministry of good men and true; but Valaoritis, though in principle not unwilling to make the attempt, saw that without support in the Chamber, and with violent hostility outside it, his position would be hopeless. Erskine heard with dismay that owing to the strenuous endeavours of his Russian colleague, Mr. Novikow, Zaïmis would, on resigning, advise the king to send for the Russian candidate Mr. Koumoundouros, under whom Zaïmis would consent to serve, with a pledge that the Dilessi Enquiry should at once be terminated. Erskine expressed to Zaïmis his astonishment that 'he [Zaïmis] was about to advise the King to send for a Minister whom he had frequently described to me as the embodiment of all that was corrupt in parliamentary government.' Zaïmis admitted that this was so; but said merely that it was a choice of evils.[1] King George, however, had his own reasons for disliking Mr. Koumoundouros, who had published some unauthorised and garbled extracts from His Majesty's correspondence in the previous April;[2] and, instead of Koumoundouros, he sent on 18 July for Mr. Deligeorgis, an astute and eloquent politician, who yet enjoyed less parliamentary support than either Zaïmis or Koumoundouros. He remained in office during the next four months.

With the change of government, the Enquiry passed into the hands of a more subtle and determined manager than Mr. Limberákis. The new public prosecutor was Mr. Papafrangos, an agile and not too scrupulous lawyer, who set about the task of arranging, along the lines indicated by Gennadios, the mass of evidence which had accumulated over the past three months. At first, the new government had some hope that their work

[1] Erskine to Granville, 13 July 1870.
[2] Erskine to Clarendon, 15 April 1870.

would be facilitated by the withdrawal of Cookson and Allan from the Enquiry. Lord Clarendon was dead, and his successor, Lord Granville, had been in office only a fortnight. Nor was this all. The assurance of the permanent under-secretary, Mr. Hammond, that the tranquillity of the international scene was disturbed only by the Greek imbroglio was followed ten days later by the outbreak of the Franco-Prussian War, which might be expected to engross the attention of the English government to the exclusion of all minor matters. Mr. Deligeorgis accordingly protested to Erskine against the continued interference of Cookson; and Erskine, now heartily sick of the whole proceeding, forwarded and supported his protest to Lord Granville. But Granville was adamant: Erskine, he minuted, had been told to insist. And on 10 August the cabinet confirmed this instruction.[1] They could not be prevailed upon to abandon the single activity, useless though it was, which showed that they were still 'doing something' in Greece.[2] And Mr. Deligeorgis, like his predecessor, was compelled to acquiesce. Mr. Papafrangos, to Cookson's surprise, showed himself cordial and accommodating; but he had his own methods of evading the Erskine-Sarávas agreement of 19 May, and he did not scruple to use them.

The Enquiry, following the route traversed by the brigands between January and April, had ranged over the five districts of Levadeia, Thebes, the Megarid, Attica and Euboea. More than five hundred persons had been examined, and more than one hundred peasants or shepherds were herded in the gaols. But this seemed insufficient to Mr. Papafrangos. He suspected that his predecessor had not elicited all that might be known of Costa Seliamis: and Seliamis was one of the principals on whom the Enquiry wished to fix responsibility for the obsti-

---

[1] B.M. Add. 44638, fol. 121.
[2] 'My own estimate . . . is that nothing has been done': Lord Carnarvon, House of Lords, Official Report, 11 July 1870.

nacy of Takos and Christos Arvanitákis. On 21 September
Papafrangos sent the commander of the Marathon gendarmerie, Adjutant Dokos, to search Seliamis' cottage at Xylokeriza. The result was surprising. Two letters, still sealed, came to
light. Both were addressed to the Arvanitákis. One came from
a brigand named Makrokostas, who was lying in prison at
Athens, and urged the gang once again to insist on a general
amnesty; the other, dated 17 April, had been written, over an
assumed name, by that very Corporal Dimitropoulos who had
accompanied the escort sent from Kato Souli on 11 April to
meet the excursionists at the well by Marathon. The contents
of the latter were, at first sight, highly incriminating. The worthy corporal introduced himself to Takos as a one-time con-
federate of some of his gang; claimed a part of the ransom to
be paid; and, in support of his claim, added very naively that if
he and his detachment had been up at the bridge of Pikermi at
the moment of the abduction, 'things which have happened
would not have happened'!

It is certain that if this letter had been shown to Cookson,
as by the terms of the agreement it ought to have been, he
would have insisted on re-opening the whole Enquiry and on
a rigorous examination in his presence of Corporal Dimitropoulos and his associates. But Mr. Papafrangos had no
intention of showing it to Cookson. Instead, he conducted his
examination of Makrokostas and Seliamis in prison at dead of
night; and the corporal was interrogated with the same secrecy. Dimitropoulos asserted that he had written the letter to
Takos with the intention of establishing personal contact with
the gang and thus contriving to be of service to the prisoners:
and this transparent excuse was accepted without question. Mr.
Papafrangos completed his digest of the evidence early in
November; but he refused to allow Cookson to see it. Not
until the printed Resolution (*Voúlevma*) of the Chambre des
mises en accusation was placed in Cookson's hands on 15

December had Cookson any idea that this epistolary evidence existed: and then it was too late to sift it to any purpose.

The circumstances touching the discovery and interpretation of these two letters remained dubious to the last. Why Mr. Papafrangos, whose duplicity, despite his lame and verbose excuses, was fully admitted in private by the Greek prime minister, should have gone to such lengths to conceal them from Cookson, is not immediately explicable. There was little to be drawn from the texts other than that a felon wanted a pardon and that a corporal was angling for some sovereigns: neither of which facts could excite much surprise. The earlier statement of Dimitropoulos, that the capture had been due to his collusion, was, on any sober appraisal, of precisely the same value as his later statement, that his letter was a device to assist the prisoners: that is to say, of no value whatever. Two explanations of Mr. Papafrangos' reticence might be suggested. The corporal's letter, at its face value, corroborated afresh all the allegations made thirteen years before by Edmond About concerning the hand-and-glove relations subsisting between brigands and gendarmerie,[1] which had been the jest of Europe ever since: and possibly Papafrangos, as a good patriot, had been unwilling to add further discredit to the already tarnished reputation of his country. But, since he did at long last release the documents, this explanation may seem not very plausible, and another may be worth consideration. It seems to have occurred to nobody at the time to question the authenticity of these two letters; yet their opportune discovery was surely such as to cast grave doubts on it. That the police should have waited five months before searching the hut of the man Seliamis, who had been in prison since April, is barely credible. And the documents themselves conveniently substantiated two of the very points which

---

[1] 'The inferences to be drawn from a demand of this sort on the part of a non-commissioned officer of the Greek army are sufficiently obvious': Erskine to Christopoulos, 22 December 1870.

the Enquiry was concerned to establish: that the brigands' insistence on amnesty between 15 and 20 April was inspired by Seliamis and some gaol-birds rather than by any more prominent personages in Athens; and that the soldiers whose account of what had passed at the well by Marathon was so damaging to Alexander Anemoyiannis were themselves of doubtful reliability. When to these facts is added the manifest reluctance of Mr. Papafrangos to submit the documents to scrutiny, and the circumstance that, despite this, they were not destroyed, the impartial observer will probably admit the possibility that at least this part of the evidence was manufactured. However it may be, Erskine told the Greek foreign minister Christopoulos that 'a fatal blow has, in my opinion, been given to the sincerity of the whole enquiry'.[1]

But the responsibility of Seliamis and his friends for the obstinacy of Takos was only a part of Mr. Papafrangos' case: and, had that obstinacy not declared itself as early as 15 April, five clear days before Mr. Noel's visit to Oropós, it would probably have been a very insignificant part. The chief of the prosecutor's ingenuity was devoted to proving that Noel, if he had not inspired, had at least strongly and deliberately reinforced that obstinacy. The young man was now, owing to the change of government, in great peril: for his local enemy, Mr. Boudouris, was cousin to the new prime minister Deligeorgis, and it was not likely that he would neglect this opportunity of pushing home his advantage. Mr. Zaïmis had been able to protect Noel, up to a point; but he had given a very clear warning that Noel should look after himself. 'Were I', said Zaïmis to Noel's friend, Michael Averoff, 'like Coumoundouro, I would bring forward twenty false witnesses, and have Noel put in prison.'[2] Mr. Papafrangos, who visited Chalkis in early September to trip up Noel's heels at a fifth interrogation, blandly assured him that 'it

---

[1] Ibid.
[2] Granville to Stuart, 22 November 1871.

would be greatly to the advantage of the Greek Government to mix up an Englishman in the matter': an admission which put the prime minister to some embarrassment, and was received with some scepticism in the English Legation.

Papafrangos went to work, with an ingenuity worthy of a better cause, on the text of the letter signed George Yannou, dated 18 April, and found on the body of the dead chieftain Christos Arvanitákis. George, as we have said, could not write: but the amanuensis was soon discovered in the person of one John Kolovós, brother of the brigands' host at Rhitsona in Boeotia. This Kolovós was in fact proved to have met George in Chalkis on 18 April. The insistence on the amnesty was brought into line with Noel's known opinion, as recorded by Herbert, that an amnesty should be given. The reference to 'settling matters on a certain day' was interpreted as a reference to the telegram from Erskine which Noel was to receive, and had received, on Tuesday, 19 April. The 'commission' which the brother chieftains were to receive without fail was the personal assurance of Noel that the government's hand could be forced. The 'koumbáros' or gossip was of course Noel himself, and the 'friends' who were urging an amnesty included him. The letter, concluded Papafrangos, had been concocted by Noel, with George and Kolovós, on 18 April, at the house of Mr. Averoff in Chalkis. Early in August a brigand named Kapsalis was taken near Lamia, and conveniently deposed that he had since heard from Takos, whose cousin he was, that Takos had stood firmly by his demands on the advice of his English 'koumbáros' who had come to him at Oropós (needless to say, Kapsalis afterwards entirely withdrew this testimony). This, together with Noel's known connexion with two of the Arvanitákis brothers, Nikolaos and Apostolis, and his supposed connexion with two more, George and Dinos, made up the case: and on 21 September Noel was formally charged at Chalkis with complicity in the abduction, and with furnishing help and advice to the Arvanitákis chiefs thereafter!

And now Noel realised to the full the danger that con-
fronted him and the helplessness of his position. He was technically liable to be clapped up there and then, pending his trial,
in Chalkis gaol, where the typhus was raging. He was, if convicted, liable to a heavy term of imprisonment, from which his
chances of emerging again were slender indeed. He was bitterly mortified that the difficulties and dangers on which he had
embarked out of a single-minded desire to help his countrymen should be so rewarded. The charge was so monstrously
unjust that it must, he believed, be manifest to all as the merest
fraud. He bombarded Erskine with letters by every post, complaining of the conspiracy of which he was the victim, and
demanding, in tones which daily became shriller and more
peremptory, the support and relief of the English Legation.[1]
But here he was soon to find what it was to have made an
enemy of his natural ally and protector. Mr. Erskine merely
'begged to observe that he should not feel justified in taking
any step of which the effect would be to deter the authorities
from proceeding against any person, whether a native or a foreigner, who may in their opinion have been concerned, however remotely, in that affair.'[2]

Noel, to whom the details of the case against him had not
as yet been disclosed, naturally concluded that much of it was
a re-hash of the charges laid three months before by his enemies Boudouris and Tombazis; and he frantically collected a
whole mass of counter-evidence which implicated them. This
evidence he passed on to Cookson; but he received an equally
frigid response. 'I could not', wrote Cookson, 'consistently with
my duty insist on the examination of the fifty or sixty indi-

[1] 'To give things their right name, his [Frank's] letters to Mr. Erskine are offen-
sive in tone, almost insolent and most improper even if Mr. Erskine were not
British Minister': Finlay to Edward Noel, 31 December 1870 (N.-B.).
[2] Erskine to Noel, 24 September 1870.

viduals whom you cite to prove that you have nothing in common with M. Boudouris. The hostility between you is an undeniable fact, admitted by that gentleman himself. If, however, among this number, or anywhere else, you can mention any witness whom you believe to be in a position to give evidence bearing in any discernible degree upon your defence, and you will be good enough to communicate to me his name and the general purport of his testimony, I will gladly undertake to press for what has already been promised me, that the examination shall not be closed until that witness has been called.'[1]

Noel had, it is true, staunch friends in de Grey and Carnarvon, who were sincerely and properly grateful to him for what he had done, at great personal risk, to save the lives of their relations. But what could they do for him? Erskine had the ear of Lord Granville, and through Lord Granville of Mr. Gladstone; and Granville perfectly agreed with Erskine's refusal to interfere in any judicial process against Noel. We blush to record that a confidential memorandum to the prejudice of Mr. Noel was compiled by an English official for the enlightenment of an English foreign secretary.[2] The object of this egregious document was to show that Frank Noel was more of a Levantine than an Englishman, and hence unworthy of trust! His mother, it was said, was 'from the East'.[3] He associated entirely with Greeks, 'going about followed by several men in fustanel dress [kilts].' His allegations against Greek judicial functionaries were partial and absurd. And his attitude to brigandage was a scandal: '. . . Mr. Noel came to Athens and those who met him at dinner at Mr. Erskine's table were surprised at the light tone in which he spoke of brigandage and of the ruf-

---

[1] Cookson to Noel, 18 October 1870.
[2] PRO F.O. 32/414, memo. of 17 November 1870.
[3] In fact, she was Frances Isabella Noel, *née* Doyle, who gave birth to him no further east than Leamington in Warwickshire. But had she come from Japan, it is not easy to discern any motive for recording the fact, other than to excite prejudice.

fians whose work we had seen.' "They [the brigands]", he said, "are the best people going." He has lived so long amongst people who look upon brigandage as quite a natural state of things that his moral sense with regard to this point may have become blunted.' To turn unsafe companion to a young gentleman at the dinner-table would appear to be evidence of a moral sense a good deal more blunted than Mr. Noel's. Such shameful usage very strikingly illustrates the wisdom of Lord Melbourne's maxim: 'You had best try to do no good, and then you will get into no scrapes.'

Deserted, as it seemed, on every hand, Frank Noel was in despair. At last he was driven to commit the unforgivable sin: on 19 December he wrote to Mr. Erskine, 'You will excuse me for feeling that I have not received in this trying case due support from Her Majesty's Legation.' Erskine was outraged. In a series of letters he demanded that Noel should substantiate or withdraw the charge. But he received no satisfaction. He forwarded Noel's accusation to Lord Granville, who passed it on to the prime minister. Mr. Gladstone commented, with characteristic sobriety: 'Mr. Noel's complaining of Erskine may be excusable under his peculiar circumstances, but I do not at present see that he has the smallest cause for it.'

Mr. Papafrangos meantime had compiled his report, and the Chambre des mises en accusation had sat on it. On 9 December they published their official findings, in the form of a lengthy Resolution or *Voúlevma*. Not a single Greek above the rank of a peasant was so much as committed; and the only persons against whom a bill was found were sixty shepherds, Costa Seliamis, George Yannou, John Kólovós, and Mr. Frank Noel. Great was the astonishment and confusion of Cookson, an astonishment and confusion which in themselves showed him to have been altogether unfit for the task he had so ill-advisedly undertaken. He saw at last that during six months he had borne the odium of his illegal position, and had striven with might and main, only to be entirely over-reached and made a laughing-stock by his agile colleagues in the Enquiry. He was acutely conscious that the result would be set down by his countrymen for the farce it was, and that he, who had not lacked the best intentions and industry, would be by them held responsible. In deep chagrin he sat down to pen a long analysis of the findings. The brothers Maléas had been acquitted by a barefaced misrepresentation of the evidence, of which Cookson had his own notes before him. The repeated statements of Herbert and Vyner that the brigands were being manipulated from Athens were got over by the simple expedient of omitting all mention of them in the Resolution. Mr. Basil Boudouris, who had been expressly implicated in the statement of the captured brigand Lioris, and Mr. Kriezotis, who had been, less directly, implicated in the giving of advice to Takos, were dismissed from the Enquiry through the opportune discovery of some individuals said to be personally hostile to them, by whom the 'slanders' against them had been set on foot. Alexander Anemoyiannis, the dragoman, rode off on some real or fancied, but in any case insignificant, discrepancies in the statements of those who had warned him at the well by Marathon, who were themselves suspect, according to the letter strangely found in the hut of Seliamis. The testimony of the brigand Lioris, and of his associate Monachos, was rejected where it touched a Greek, but accepted where it touched those whom the Chamber wished to implicate. In short, Cookson gravely concluded,

> the unavoidable results of the whole matter therefore seem to be that while on the one hand the investigations will have failed in bringing to justice any of the persons with a view to whose discovery and conviction Her Majesty's Government first insisted on what the Greek lawyers consider a violation of the criminal procedure of the country, on the other hand the only reparation which was demanded of the Greek Government will not have been satisfactorily rendered,

as the enquiry cannot be said to have been conducted with that impartiality and disregard of personal or political motives which were required and promised.[1]

Such naivete is too exasperating to be pathetic. But Cookson had at least been taught one lesson: he requested that his analysis of the Resolution should not be published. After all, what was the use?

As for Mr. Noel, he had had too much of the follies of Erskine and Cookson to rely on them for any further assistance. He briefed his own Greek lawyers, and sent his case to the Court of Appeal without further ado. He was, to be sure, taken somewhat aback by the advice of his legal friends, who urged him to put forward whatever might conduce to his exculpation, whether it were true or false; and he had great difficulty in confining them to the truth, to which they appeared to be totally indifferent. But, in fact, the Greek authorities had never had any intention of sentencing Noel, as a man of wider experience than his would have seen from the start. The 'ethnic' champions were concerned merely to put on record that the Dilessi murders were the work of foreigners: and, this done, they had no interest in persecuting Noel any further. On 28 January 1871 the Appeal Court, while emphasising the weight of the circumstantial evidence against him, found themselves unable to decide whether Noel was or was not the 'koumbáros' mentioned in George Yannou's letter; and they therefore suspended the proceedings against him *sine die*. Finlay professed to see in this decision an intention to keep the charge hanging over Noel's head in case he should be troublesome in future. The Court had probably no such intention. Now that Greece was officially and totally absolved from all guilt in the affair, it was a matter of indifference to her what might become of Frank Noel. 'Although', he wrote to his father, 'I thought I was

[1] Cookson to Erskine, 4 February 1871.

pretty well acquainted with the Greek character, I find to my cost that up to the present time I knew nothing. If I had been told a few days back that it was possible to find people to give utterance to such dastardly calumny I would not have believed it.' We live and learn.

The English government also, preoccupied as they were with far weightier matters at home and abroad, yet found time to be shocked both at the concealment of the letters entrusted to Seliamis and at the general result of the Enquiry. 'The Greek Government', said Mr. Gladstone, 'appears to be implicated in a gross breach of faith, and the subject matter in which it has been committed seems to be so important as to vitiate the authority of the inquiry.'[1] At the opening of Parliament on 9 February, the Speech from the Throne contained a passage which expressed, temperately enough, the government's dissatisfaction with the results of the investigation and their intention to pursue it further. The Greek public learnt of this reflexion with the bitterest resentment. The outcry was scarcely less noisy than that which the murders themselves had provoked. It appeared that Greece could not be content with her own official exoneration unless everybody else made a show of believing in it also. The indignation seems artificial and exaggerated until we remember that the official verdict of the Enquiry had now become an article in the canon of 'ethnic' truth, which it must therefore be heretical and criminal to call in question.

It is painful to continue this absurd story. Lord Granville, hot on the scent of Corporal Dimitropoulos' letter to Takos, was convinced that its thorough sifting would lead to the detection of some deep conspiracy. In this he was manifestly wrong, since the corporal had been acting on his own account and nobody else's. Nonetheless, Granville demanded that the Enquiry should be re-opened. The Greek pundits declared that

---

[1] Gladstone to Granville, 7 January 1871: *Political Correspondence of Mr. Gladstone and Lord Granville 1868–76*, ed. Ramm, I (London, 1952), 207.

this was illegal. A separate investigation into the activities of Corporal Dimitropoulos personally could be allowed; but at no point must this investigation touch any person or persons exonerated by the official Resolution. Even Granville saw that with these limitations such an enquiry would be farcical. He forbade Cookson and Allan to have any part in it; and for this removal of the hated interlopers the new prime minister, Mr. Koumoundouros, appropriated the credit. The special Enquiry sat for nearly a whole year, and at last reached the not very surprising conclusion that there were no grounds for proceeding further against Corporal Dimitropoulos. 'It seems to me', wrote Finlay, 'that Erskine is blundering again in making a fuss about the letter of the gendarme Petro Demetropoulos, which was never delivered, and which, if it had been, would now be of no consequence.'[1] The only interesting feature of this vain and misguided re-opening of the investigation was a side-issue.

To preside over it was set, at Erskine's instigation, a judge named 'Rocco Coïdan' (Rokkos Choïdás).[2] Erskine, misinformed as usual, supposed this person to be a native of the Ionian Islands (in fact, he was born at Nauplia in the Morea), and therefore more likely to be trustworthy, that is to say, pro-English. But the very fact that Erskine placed confidence in an Ionian Greek is not without historical interest: for it shows that, contrary to what Greek propaganda had maintained up to the cession of the islands in 1863, there had been in those islands a respectable minority friendly to the English Protectorate. Spyridon Valaoritis and Peter Braila were notable representatives of this minority, as were the poet Dionysios Solomós and his brother Dimitrios; although none of them, except perhaps the last, had wished this Protectorate to continue. It is not very probable that, in our own day, a British ambassador in Athens would regard it as an advantage to Great Britain that the judge

[1] Finlay to Edward Noel, 20 January 1871 (N.-B.).
[2] Erskine to Granville, 9 March 1871.

in an Anglo-Greek dispute should be of Cypriot extraction.

The trial of those committed by the Resolution of 9 December, with the exception of Frank Noel, whom the Appeal Court had exempted, was fixed for 1 May 1871. But meanwhile the tale of poor Mr. Erskine's blunderings was told. During twelve months, owing to the mistaken insistence of Gladstone and the English Foreign Office, he had been kept at his post, in spite of a suggestion from Queen Victoria that he should be removed.[1] He had borne in Athens a burden of unpopularity which even his incompetence did not wholly deserve; and the publication by the Foreign Office of all his dispatches and enclosures as soon as they were received, except for a very few passages in those which he begged might remain confidential, added to his difficulties. In this series of publications appeared, not only the startling disclosure of Mr Zaïmis, but also Erskine's own expressed belief that all Greeks were liars, and his statement that he put little confidence in any promise given him by a Greek minister Remarks of this kind, made in private conversation or correspondence, should of course never have been printed; and in addition to suffering for his own faults, Erskine was made to suffer also for the indiscretions of Clarendon and Otway and Hammond.

At last, in April 1871, the strain became unbearable. On the 8th of that month he telegraphed to Granville that an attack had completely prostrated his nervous system, and he begged for two months' leave. A week later, having received no reply to his application, he left hurriedly and without sanction for Trieste. 'Mr. Erskine's health,' wrote the chargé, Mr. Watson, 'in consequence of the prolonged anxiety which he had undergone, was such as, in the opinion of his medical adviser, to necessitate an immediate change of scene.' Rumour was rife in Athens that he was out of his mind, and rumour was, for once,

---

[1] Cabinet of 13 June 1870: 'Queen's suggestion for the removal of Erskine.' (B.M. Add. 44638, fol. 88.)

very nearly accurate.[1] He hastened from Trieste to Vienna, and from Vienna to Salzburg. But his letters to Lord Granville remained unanswered. His place however was quickly supplied. Mr. Stuart was summoned from Buenos Aires; and, after a lengthy briefing by Lord Granville, arrived in Athens on 10 May.

The English government, largely through their own ignorance and folly, had been duped all round. The labouring mountains had produced nothing but a rat. But there was still one way in which pressure could be exerted on Greece, a most unworthy and ignoble way, to which the English government now resorted. Julia Lloyd had by her husband's death been left destitute, and worse than destitute: for Edward Lloyd had died £1,500 in debt. King George, in the kindness of his heart, had at once presented her with £1,000 and had promised that she should be provided for: a promise later confirmed by Mr. Deligeorgis. The matter had been in abeyance since the death of Lord Clarendon; but now Granville took it up with energy. A demand was made of the prime minister, Mr. Koumoundouros, that Greece should pay over the sum of £10,000 for Mrs. Lloyd's settlement. The sum, equal to at least £40,000 of our money today, was on any reckoning exorbitant; and Greece was one of the poorest countries in Europe. Mrs. Lloyd had already received £1,000, which had been increased to £3,000 by the generous donations of Greek merchants in London and Manchester. Moreover, of the children for whom she had to provide only the daughter Barbara was Lloyd's, the rest being offspring of a previous marriage. But these considerations were mere trifles in comparison with the fact that she was by no law entitled to a shilling of compensation from Greece. No country can accept financial responsibility for crimes committed with-

---

[1] *Mérimna*, 15 April 1871. The sensational story recorded by Watbled (103– 4, note) that, at the funeral of the Italian minister Della Minerva, Erskine had been sprinkled by blood from the corpse and had at once collapsed, is, like some other parts of Watbled's narrative, apocryphal: Della Minerva's funeral took place on 10 April, two days after Erskine's announcement of his nervous prostration.

in its borders. And if the sum were paid, this would imply acceptance by Greece of responsibility for the crime itself.

As might have been expected, Mr. Gladstone had been very doubtful as to the justice of this demand. He thought £10,000 far too much. An annuity of £400 per annum could be purchased for half the sum; and this, with the £3,000 in cash already subscribed, should suffice. But Lord de Grey insisted. He felt that only the lump sum, paid over to English trustees and invested in English four per cents, would meet the case. Gladstone, who had wished to make it a cabinet issue, flinched from a collision with the Lord President, whose own cruel bereavement entitled him to much consideration. He therefore withdrew his opposition, and said he should be willing to concur in whatever Lord Granville decided.

Granville, exasperated by the Enquiry and egged on by Mrs. Lloyd, pressed his demand. The king had promised that provision should be made, and made it must be. Mr. Koumoundouros, who has not hitherto appeared before us in the most favourable of lights, had nonetheless many statesman-like qualities; and, seeing that the time was now come when Dilessi must be buried and forgotten, he undertook, in the teeth of violent opposition, to push through a bill authorising the payment. In vain did Mr. Milisis, in a speech lasting four hours,[1] review every aspect of the Dilessi affair, drench the luckless Mr. Zaïmis in torrents of scorn, and prove beyond all question that the proposed grant to the widow was an unjustifiable extortion and a pernicious precedent. Mr. Koumoundouros, with excellent sense and moderation, merely said that the sum was an ex-gratia payment to a poor woman who had suffered undeservedly in their country, and he appealed to the generosity and good-nature of the House to sanction it. The bill was passed by a surprisingly large majority.

[1] Milisis, *Two Speeches*. This speech was made on 19 May 1871, and is the best summary of the final 'ethnic' position on Dilessi.

In August the money was finally paid. The minister of finance, who made the payment, was Mr. Sotiropoulos, the one-time prisoner of Laphazanis. It may be imagined with what feelings he surrendered this princely compensation to a fellow-sufferer, while he himself, five years before, had been reduced to destitution.

The trial of the accused of Dilessi began in May, and lasted six weeks. It is unnecessary to follow it in detail. The prisoners, finally reduced to fifty in number, were tried in five batches, according to their places of origin. Those from Levadeia, who were Vlachs, the judge virtually directed the jury to convict; those from Thebes and the Megarid, who were Greeks, he no less clearly directed them to acquit.[1] It was, however, very plain that in the large majority of cases justice should be tempered with mercy. The guilt, if guilt it were, of harbouring and supplying the brigands was brought home to most of the defendants; but their plea of *vis major* was rightly urged and rightly accepted. Among the accused of Attica the man Bobis spoke up powerfully in his own defence. The government, he said, might mean very well. But, if peasants like himself were required to repulse and inform against brigands, how could the government protect them and their families from the vengeance of the gangs? For a quarter of an hour's enforced entertainment of the Arvanitákis, he had lain six months without trial in gaol. On his liberation, he would take his wife and children with him across the border into Turkey. And who shall blame him? In this batch Costa Seliamis and the luckless Goggos were prominent; and although the latter was implicated solely on the evidence of the captive brigand Lioris, and although Lioris now roundly denied ever having given such evidence, Goggos, with Seliamis, was found guilty and sentenced to life imprisonment. These men were cat's-paws, who did not deserve such harsh treatment; and it is to be hoped, and believed, that the

[1] Cookson to Stuart, 15 June 1871.

sentence was not carried out in full upon them.

On 27 May came the turn of the accused of Chalkis, principally of George Yannou Arvanitákis and John Kolovós, said to have been his amanuensis. With a skill which astonished Mr. Cookson, the counsel for Kolovós argued him out of any complicity in the affair, and he was set free. George Yannou, though by the acquittal of Kolovós his authorship of the letter to Takos and Christos was made even more uncertain, and though by Noel's testimony he had taken no part whatsoever in the negotiations between Theagenis and Takos on 20 April, was nonetheless convicted and sentenced to five years' imprisonment. Of the remainder, eleven Vlachs were given nominal terms of detention. The other thirty-six peasants were discharged.

This was officially the end of the matter.

> The result of this last trial [wrote Cookson] is that we are now as far as ever from knowing who wrote the notorious letter from Chalcis, or who are the friends mentioned therein as assuring George Arvanitakis that the amnesty could be granted, or who was the 'Coumbáro' with whom the brigand chiefs were to communicate if their brother did not come to them as he expected.[1]

There is a children's game called fox-and-geese. In it the fox, a black pawn on a chess-board, tries to break through a cordon of four white pawns, the geese. As each alley-way opens to the fox, his opponent adroitly blocks it with a goose. Cookson, a very goose-like fox, suffered the same treatment from a flock of very fox-like geese: until at last, with every avenue barred, he was driven into a corner and right off the board by the flapping, hissing gaggle around him. The last word on these tactics may be left to Finlay: 'Some members of the Government felt alarm for their nearest connections and were acute enough to see that the safest thing for those in the highest places was for the enquiry to run wild in every direction, so

[1] Cookson to Stuart, 3 June 1871.

that it should end in a confusion of useful knowledge.'[1] From this point of view, the Enquiry may be regarded as a complete success.

[1] Finlay to Edward Noel, 19 November 1870 (N.-B.).

# CHAPTER EIGHT

# 'TRÈS VRAISEMBLABLE...'

'We shall perhaps never know the true history of this unhappy affair.'

GRAPHIC, 7 MAY 1870

By the spring of 1871 there was scarcely anybody in either England or Greece who was not sick to death of the whole untidy affair; and elsewhere almost everybody had forgotten it. Events of incomparably greater moment, in France, in Germany, in Russia and Italy, even in England herself, had long ago intervened to drive it from the foreground of interest. Of those more directly concerned, Noel had been dismissed from the case, Erskine was languishing half-demented in Austria, Papafrangos had been sent to exercise his talents at Nauplia, and Mr. Koumoundouros, now prime minister, had introduced some, on paper, admirable measures for the extermination of brigandage.[1] Even the persistent George Finlay was urging that the matter should now be dropped. Greece, satisfied by the official findings of her own Enquiry that she had been perfectly innocent and wantonly gibbeted by the Pilates of Europe, was turning with relief to the affairs of the Roux-Serpieri Company, which was all too successfully exploiting the lead and silver mines at Lavrion.

The Enquiry, as we have seen, had been a masterpiece in the art of 'covering up'. The tactics adopted were to elicit sev-

[1] On 11 March 1871. Cookson was sceptical as to their value: he appositely quoted, *'Quid leges sine moribus Vanae proficiunt?'*

eral dozen contradictory accounts of the same transaction. In this way, though several persons might be implicated, very few could be convicted, since no statement was on record which was not either withdrawn by the deponent himself or else controverted by some other deponent of as much, or as little, authority.

In such a state of confusion it was easy for the assessors to accept or reject any parts they might choose of testimonies such as those of Lioris or Seliamis, which, according to the various versions given by these deponents, might be considered equally true or false. When we add to this confusion the fact that extreme caution and secrecy were, for obvious reasons, preserved by the more prominent citizens in their contacts with brigands, we shall not fail to agree with the dictum of the Austrian minister Haymerle: 'It will be extremely hard to establish juridical proofs against any persons of note, who employ subaltern agents in these affairs. The general impunity . . . is too much in the interest of everybody to allow of any revelations of importance.'[1]

Is it then possible, at this distance of time, to establish with at least a fair amount of probability the main course of the Dilessi intrigue? It appears to us as some long sunken wreck might appear to a diver on the sea-floor: the outlines blurred by the gloomy medium and by the accretion of innumerable flora and fauna of the marine; yet still recognisable for what it once was, still showing the salient features of the original merchantman or ship of war.

That the capture was exploited, and the brigands' subsequent conduct directed, by some person or persons of influence in Athens, we have seen to be indisputable. Perhaps the only evidence in the whole affair which can be regarded as entirely disinterested and candid was that of the victims them-

[1] Haymerle to Beust, 14 May 1870 (Bibliography no.8).

selves: quite apart from their personal integrity, which could not be questioned even by Gennadios, they had nothing whatever to gain by misrepresenting the truth. Now, Herbert explicitly stated that Takos was in receipt of letters from Athens which governed both his policy and his temper. In connexion with this vital matter of communications from Athens, we must notice also the evidence of a member of the gang, Apostolos Karavidas, who was captured at Kaïtza by the Turkish authorities on 14 November 1870. Cookson saw the importance of interrogating this prisoner before his extradition to Greece, and he hasted to Larissa for the purpose. On 25 November Karavidas was examined, in the presence of Rifaat Pasha, the Mutessarif, by Cookson and by the dragoman to the English vice-consulate at Larissa. The prisoner confirmed that Takos had received news that 'the amnesty would be granted' before he proceeded to Oropós (that is to say, he received it on the night of Thursday, 14 April); and went on to describe another communication which had reached the band on 19 April and had reinforced their obstinacy. The interrogation ran thus:

Q. Where did your chiefs get the assurance of their pardon?
A. From a letter they had received.
Q. Where did they receive the letter from?
A. They did not produce it: how should I know?
Q. Have they discussed on the purport of the letter?
A. They all met at one place and read it. They subsequently burnt it; and, asking what the letter contained, I was told that the pardon will be granted.
Q. Who burnt the letter?
A. Christo, Arvanitaki's brother that was killed.
Q. Did you see him burn it?
A. Yes, I saw him.
Q. Did you receive the letter before or after you fought

with the troops?

A. On our arrival at Oropó, two days before the fight . . .

Q. Was it before or after the day the letter was burnt that Yorghi Yanouli [George Yannou] came there?

A. Before.

Now, if this letter came two days before 21 April and also after the arrival of George Yannou, who, as we know, reached Oropós late on the evening of 19 April, it is no very bold conjecture that George was himself the bearer of it; and doubtless its contents were identical with that 'commission which you must by all means receive', to which George had referred in his letter to Takos and Christos of 18 April. The vital letter which was read and then burnt by Christos therefore contained a final confirmation of what Takos had been assured by the two mysterious emissaries on 14 April. It is not demonstrably certain that this letter emanated from Athens; but it can be said that no letter from Athens could have reached Oropós by a more direct route than Chalkis, since on and after 15 April Mr. Zaïmis had closed the land routes to the brigands for all except official traffic. The letter was unsigned; and yet it had carried such weight with the chiefs that nothing said on the morrow by Theagenis could prevail against it. The writer was therefore a person of the highest importance in their eyes: in short, their political director and impresario. The captured brigand Lioris, at his latest examination, had given the name of Mr. Basil Boudouris of Euboea as the forwarder of this, or of some other, decisive letter. Now it is only fair to Boudouris to say that Karavidas was twice given an opportunity to corroborate the testimony of Lioris, and altogether failed to do so. Nor is it at all probable that Takos would have relied so implicitly on the assurance of even so prominent a personage as Boudouris, unless it had been supported by a higher authority still, the authority of that 'someone in the background at Athens.'

Suspicions at Athens fell first on General Soutzos; but soon afterwards, with better reason, on the powerful chief of the Opposition, Alexander Koumoundouros.[1] These suspicions, whether well or ill-founded, at least did no injustice to that statesman's general reputation. Every circumstance of past career and present incentive could tell against him. He was a Greek politician of the old school, able and determined, who exploited to the full, without ruth or scruple, such means as lay to his hand. His name, more perhaps than that of any other politician, had been since 1862 connected with the employment of banditti. In January 1865 he had procured the acquittal of a notorious brigand and brigand-harbourer, Vasilis Tzelios, who was bound to him by ties closer than those of political expediency: for Tzelios was betrothed to the sister of one Andreas Stratos, and Stratos himself was offering for Miss Koumoundouros. Such a state of affairs scarcely admitted of caricature, even by traducers like Edmond About: let them write what they would, the truth still outran them. The reputation of Koumoundouros in this respect was so dark that in 1865 the prime minister, Admiral Kanaris, referred with contempt to his own minister of the interior as 'that brigand Koumoundouros'. He had during the Cretan rebellion of 1866–67 employed brigand bands to invade the Turkish province of Thessaly and to provoke 'spontaneous uprisings' among its Christian population. It was he who, on his own admission, had been the principal in negotiating with brigand chiefs, including Takos, for the amnestying, enrolment and dispatch to Crete of one hundred brigands in 1867. Nor was his conduct during and after the capture and murder of Herbert's party such as in any way to allay suspicion. It is true that during the crucial days of April he allowed it to be known that he had retired to bed with some unspecified complaint.[2] Yet there

---

[1] LHéritier, 330.
[2] *Palingenesia*, 14 April 1870.

was the direct, though undisclosed, evidence of the man Seliamis that on a day which we saw reason to believe must have been Saturday, 16 April, he had carried to Athens a letter from Takos addressed to Koumoundouros personally. His subsequent proceedings betrayed his motives but too clearly. He was the party chief to whom the Megarian brothers Maléas adhered; and these brothers had quite certainly employed the Arvanitákis gang during the municipal elections of 28 March 1870. It was Koumoundouros who moved heaven and earth to exculpate them: and was, said Mr. Erskine, 'violently opposed to the continuance of the judicial enquiry, by which several of his own supporters are seriously compromised . . .'[1] The cool and cynical opportunism which he had displayed in his conversation with Sir Henry Elliot on 4 May showed that he regarded the whole business as a political manoeuvre, which he was only too ready to exploit for party purposes.

Yet two circumstances are to be borne in mind. In the first place, it cannot be said that such a manoeuvre was beyond the power of any but Koumoundouros to devise. His rival, Dimitrios Bulgaris, possessed an invention equally fertile and a character even less scrupulous. King George in later life recalled that on the eve of a general election in the 1870s Bulgaris had openly advocated the murder of his most prominent rival.[2] But with the Marathon capture there was no evidence at all, even circumstantial, to connect Bulgaris, though he was as ready as anyone else to profit by the political upheaval. Secondly, it must once again be stressed that while everyone asserted and believed that the capture was a political job, no one for a second imagined that its contrivers foresaw or desired its fatal consequence. The direct responsibility for this lay with Zaïmis

[1] Erskine to Granville, 13 July 1870.
[2] Prince Nicholas, 77; who, however, states that the rival in question was Kolettis. King George must have known, and his son should have known, that Kolettis died in 1847. The person whom Bulgaris wished to put out of the way was probably Koumoundouros himself.

and Erskine, and, to a less extent, with their agent Theagenis. Those who manipulated Takos concluded merely that England would unhesitatingly force the hand of Zaïmis, who would yield, resign and make way for the opposition. The prisoners would be liberated, and every one, except the Zaïmis faction, would be happy. Their error was that of those Pharisees and Sadducees who could not discern the signs of the times. They mistook Mr. Gladstone for Lord Palmerston.

As for the capture itself, this might be concerted easily enough. The intention of Herbert to take a party of travellers to Marathon on Monday, 11 April, was communicated to the police by Mr. Lambros on the previous Saturday: and this implies that it was known to everyone in Athens by Saturday night, and probably to most people in Attica by midday on Sunday. There was plenty of time for any interested parties in Athens to communicate with Takos and Christos, who, as we know from the evidence of Karavidas, were at this time absent from the band, and may even have been in Athens itself. In this connexion we should have welcomed some more detailed information as to the movements of their cattle-dealing broth-er Dinos between 9 and 11 April: for, on the evidence of one of the captured brigands, the chiefs expected the arrival of 'one of their brothers from Athens', with whose help their plans were to be laid.

The part played in the abduction by the dragoman Alexan-der is one of the most puzzling features of the whole episode. He had from the first been suspected by both Erskine and Clarendon; and he was certainly a most untrustworthy agent and witness. He had in 1855, during the Anglo-French occu-pation of Piraeus, been more than suspected of plotting with brigands to murder Commissary Strickland and to pillage the Commissariat chest. He had since then twice fallen into the hands of brigands while conducting English excursionists. In the Marathon affair, he had denied the evidence of Kamboutzis as to the repeated warnings given at the well; and he had insisted that the party should return to Athens on the same road by which they had come. He was evidently known to the Arvanitákis, who treated him with cordial familiarity; and he consorted with them more than with the captives. According to the evidence of Colonel Theagenis, he had betrayed to Takos the substance of a conversation held in the Italian language between the Colonel, Herbert and de Boÿl. He had, it was true, said to the prisoners, 'If they kill you, they may as well kill me too, as, if you die, my livelihood is gone'; but this was no proof of innocence, since there was at that time no question of killing, and in any case the event belied his words. Finally, the Enquiry had been at peculiar pains to exonerate him from all blame, which was consistent with an apprehension on somebody's part of what he might have to tell if he were put on his trial. These, and other, circumstances justified the hypothesis that Alexander had led his charges into a trap. Yet, in sum, they did not amount to a clear case against him. The prisoners themselves had not ventured to accuse him of complicity; and Erskine after a close examination, was inclined to give him the benefit of the doubt.[1]

Suspicions converging on Koumoundouros as the prime mover in the affair later suggested to the French historian LHéritier that a yet darker intrigue lay behind.[2] Applying the simple test of *cui bono*, LHéritier rightly saw that only one of the Powers had gained, and gained handsomely, by the disaster, and that Power was Russia. The leader of the so-called 'Russian-Orthodox' party in Athens was Koumoundouros himself, and LHéritier very plainly stated his conviction that the *enlève-ment* was not simply a move in the Greek political game, but concerted with the active instigation and support of the Russian Legation in Athens.

[1] Erskine to Clarendon, 29 April 1870.
[2] LHéritier, 321–361.

The circumstantial evidence for this bold hypothesis was undoubtedly very strong. Since 1867 Russian policy in the Balkans had been the policy known as Panslavism: that is to say, domination by Russia to be secured through the awakening of Slav national consciousness in this area and through the liberation of Slav populations from Greek Orthodox and Turkish political control. The protagonist in this political drama was General Ignatiew, the Russian ambassador in Constantinople. The first step was to sever the Bulgarian Church from its dependence on the Greek Œcumenical Patriarchate, and to found in Bulgaria an autonomous national communion under a Bulgarian 'exarch'. It was not to be expected that this would be tamely borne by the Greek Church; and the patriarch of Constantinople declared himself resolutely opposed to it. But Russian intrigue was more than amatch for him. Pressure was put on the Sultan, who, on 11 March 1870, exactly one month before the Marathon abduction, issued a 'firman' establishing the Bulgarian Exarchate in all territories inhabited, or mainly inhabited, by Bulgarians.

The policy of Panslavism was in direct opposition to that which had been favoured by every Greek politician since the liberation. It was the firm belief of all Greeks that Greece herself was the reversionary of the crumbling Othoman Empire, to which she laid claim in virtue of historical right and cultural superiority. Different theories obtained in Athens as to how this great consummation would come about: some put their trust in the eventual and inevitable rise to supreme power of the Greek element within the empire itself, some looked to western philhellenism; some still believed that Russia, the Orthodox child of Byzantium, would step in to restore the throne of the East to her Orthodox Greek brethren: and this strange delusion had survived even the publication in 1854 of conversations between the Tsar Nicholas and Sir Hamilton Seymour, in which His Imperial Majesty had declared, with much force of language, that Russia had not the smallest intention of helping Greece to restore the Empire of the Bosphorus. But, whatever were to be the means, that such was the ultimate destiny of Greece no Greek doubted for a moment

The Panslavic programme was therefore bound to arouse bitter Greek hostility; and it was, from 1867 onwards, the task of Russian diplomacy to lull Greek suspicions and to prevent Greece from casting herself irretrievably into the arms of the rival Protectors, England and France. In 1867 the Cretan revolt against Turkey was still alight; and Russia, who on principle favoured any diminution of the Othoman power, gave unambiguous signs that she approved, and some hints that she might further, Greek policy in that island. But when in 1869 it became clear even to russophil Greeks that Russia was a broken reed and that she would join with the other Powers at Paris in rivetting afresh the Turkish bonds on Crete, then at last Greek eyes were opened to what was going on to the north of them, and a wave of anti-Russian sentiment flooded the public and press.[1]

The Russian minister in Athens, Mr. Novikow, was seriously alarmed. King George, for all his Russian wife, was turning very decidedly in the opposite direction. In January 1870 he quarrelled violently with Mr. Koumoundouros, the 'homme de La Russie.' And when the king persuaded Mr. Valaoritis, whose western and anti-Russian sentiments were notorious, to become foreign minister, Novikow was near to despair. He was, wrote his Austrian colleague in February, *'dans une excitation continuelle de crainte de ne pas faire assez pour les intérêts de la Russie'*. He wrote a dispatch, the substance of which his government allowed to appear in a Trieste newspaper, violently attacking King George and stating that the king's position, owing altogether to his own incapacity, was nearly untenable. And rumours were afloat in Petersburg that the king was ill-treating his Russian queen.

[1] Haymerle to Beust, 28 February 1870 (Bibliography no. 8).

It is at this crisis in Russo-Greek relations – when Novikow is urging on the king, with whom he is scarcely on speaking terms, the return to power of the russophil Koumoundouros, and the king has stated that if he has again to send for that statesman, he shall take very good care to limit his opportunities for mischief-making; when, under Russian pressure, the Sultan has torn the Bulgarian Church from the control of the Greek Patriarch, and the Greek Patriarch has, with approval from Athens, stated that he shall not recognise the Sultan's fiat – it is at this precise conjuncture that an event takes place which in a moment opens a wide and enduring breach between Greece and the most powerful, the most anti-Russian, of her western allies, and throws her, willy-nilly, upon the protection of Russia herself! Small wonder if LHéritier, while admitting that he 'had found no proof . . . which discovers the complicity of the Russian Legation in the Oropós affair', was yet constrained to add, 'et cependant, il est très vraisemblable que . . . l'idée vint des agents du tsar, ou que du moins ils l'encouragèrent.'[1]

These are deep waters. We seem to be transported from the world of practical diplomacy into that of sensational fiction: into that of Joseph Conrad's *The Secret Agent,* with Novikow playing, far more adroitly and successfully, the part of Mr. Vladimir. That any concrete evidence directly implicating Novikow should one day come to light, is most improbable. LHéritier, who, by means which he prudently abstained from divulging, had obtained access to a large number of Russian diplomatic documents of this epoch, found no such evidence: nor was this to be expected. The coup of Novikow, if his it were, must have been of his own devising, since the shortness of time during which such a scheme must be set on foot would have precluded any previous consultation with his government.

Needless to say, LHéritier was not the first to propound this theory, though his was the first reasoned formulation of it to

[1] LHéritier, 342.

appear in print. Contemporary English radicals, especially, who were willing to believe everything bad of the Tsar's government, regarded Russian complicity as a matter of course. Mr. Isaac Ironside, chairman of the 'Foreign Affairs Committee of Sheffield', expressed the belief in a memorial to Lord Clarendon: 'It is not necessary to inform Your Lordship that the same power which causes all the troubles in Greece, is the same that is moving in the present troubles, although not seen. . . . She is silent as the grave, although secretly indulging in fiendish delight at her work.'[1]

Whatever might be the truth concerning Russian participation in the capture, there is overwhelming evidence that the Tsar's government regarded it as a god-send, and exploited it to the full both in Greece and Europe. The Russian press was the only press in Europe, not excepting that of Greece, which wholeheartedly espoused the cause of the Greek government. A Petersburg newspaper stated that the victims had only themselves to blame for their fate, since nobody had compelled them to go on the trip to Marathon. A Moscow newspaper, commenting on the Commons debate of 20 May, observed that 'Russia will never tolerate a change in the fundamental ordinances of Greece at the behest of Palmer and Bulwer'. We have already noted the strong démarche made by Brunnow to Lord Claren don on 15 May, and the capital made of it by Gortchakow on the following day.

In Athens Novikow worked indefatigably to frustrate any concerted attempt on the part of his colleagues to put pressure on the Greek government;[2] to stop the Enquiry at the earliest possible moment; and to effect a reconciliation between Zaïmis and Koumoundouros, with the aim of bringing the latter to

---

[1] Isaac Ironside to Clarendon, 24 June 1870.
[2] Haymerle to Beust, 24 April 1870 (Bibliography no. 8). Novikow stated that any such attempt would be 'an interference in the internal affairs of Greece.' The words have a familiar ring.

power. Such energy did not go unrewarded by his august Master. On 31 May one of the newspapers of the Koumoundouros group announced that Mr. Novikow had been promoted to be ambassador at Vienna, one of the three most important Russian posts in Europe; and followed the announcement with a eulogy of Novikow and of his political friends in Greece.

When, at the end of the year 1870, Mr. Koumoundouros did at length recover power, Novikow had been translated to this more exalted sphere. Once firmly in the saddle, Koumoundouros set about distributing the plums to his principal supporters. To Mr. Charilaos Trikoupis he offered the Legation at Constantinople; and seemed surprised and hurt when the Porte declared that Trikoupis, a very rancorous enemy of Turkey, was *persona non grata*. The Petersburg Legation was given to Mr. Boudouris—not the Basil Boudouris of Euboean fame, but his cousin Dimitrios, who had been foreign minister in 1864. To this appointment no objection was raised. Boudouris, on arrival, presented his credentials to the Tsar Alexander in person. His Imperial Majesty took occasion to observe that Mr. Koumoundouros was the only statesman capable of governing Greece at the present time, and to urge the importance of his retention in office. He added, that he had spoken in the same sense to King George, during the latter's recent visit to Russia.[1]

---

[1] Stuart to Granville, 29 September 1871.

# CHAPTER NINE

# WHAT CAME OF IT AT LAST

They mourn, but smile at length; and, smiling, mourn...
The day drags through, though storms keep out the sun;
And thus the heart will break, and brokenly live on.

### CHILDE HAROLD'S PILGRIMAGE

The derisory results of so much toil and pain in the Enquiry
led the English to suppose that Greece, by her adroit manipu-
lation of the evidence, had come scatheless out of the affair. But
this was far from the truth. Greece, whether she deserved it or
not, was the chief sufferer, and her sufferings were prolonged.
She had founded her pretension to supremacy in the Near East
on the boast of her superior civilisation. The exposure which
followed the Dilessi tragedy at once made it clear that, so far
from being fit to govern an empire, she was unable or unwilling to prevent the most barbarous outrages within a few
leagues of her own capital city. It was revealed to the world that
brigandage 'had connexions in every rank of society, from the
peasant and the trader to the senator and the priest';[1] and, worst
of all, Greece came off in this respect very badly by comparison with the despised Othomans, whom she was claiming the
right to supplant.[2] Public opinion in Europe generally echoed
the sentiment expressed by Lord Clarendon:[3] 'It is a scandal to
civilisation and an offence to the Powers who called Greece
into existence as an independent State, and as such have pro-

[1] Finlay to Edward Noel, 19 November 1870 (N.-B.).
[2] See *Revue des deux mondes*, May 1870, 255.
[3] Clarendon to Erskine, 28 April 1870; cf. Townshend, viii.

183

tected her, that, after the lapse of more than forty years, such things should occur.' It was the opinion of the Greek chargé at Paris, Mr. Rokkos, that a mortal blow had been struck at Greek national interests. The truth was, that the whole nation was made to suffer for the conduct of a few disreputable politicians: 'and this', wrote Burnouf, 'is acknowledged by all honest Greeks, for I hear on all sides the opinion that their country will never rehabilitate herself in the world's esteem unless she succeeds in escaping out of the hands of certain ambitious persons who are in the public eye and by whose conduct the whole of Greece is judged.'[1] The disease was more easily diagnosed than remedied. The power of the political chiefs was so widely and so firmly based, and their methods of government so traditional, as to allow of no alternative except in name: and many years were to elapse before any significant improvement was discernible. Yet, by men of insight and wisdom, it was rightly seen that no reforms imposed on Greece from outside could be of any avail, and that she must be left to work out her own salvation.

Outstanding among such men of wisdom was Mr. Gladstone. His conduct presented a shining example of justice and courage, humanity and common sense. His resistance to the hysterical demands for 'action' in Greece was no doubt made easier in the cabinet by the secret menaces of Prince Gortchakow. Yet it is certain that Gladstone had rejected any idea of forcible intervention long before these threats were uttered. As early as 30 April, the Austrian minister at Athens observed satirically: 'Musurus Pasha seemed to think an English occupation possible. This no doubt would be an act of kindness to Greece; yet it is hard to believe that any government, let alone Mr. Gladstone's, would be disposed to sacrifice men and money in order to give peace and security to this country.' Alexander Vyzantios spoke more worthily: 'Mr. Gladstone's

[1] Burnouf, 992.

affection for Greece was proof against all disappointment; and after the Dilessi massacre he, then prime minister, resisted the senseless assault of public opinion, and regarded only one atonement as worthy of English acceptance: that the blood of his countrymen should be the inspiration of Greece to rid herself of the stain of brigandage.' Gladstone, wiser than his contemporaries, knew that the sad internal state of Greece was but the temporary outcome of her sudden liberation from the house of bondage; and that 'there is only one cure for the evils which newly acquired freedom produces; and that cure is freedom.'

In the same spirit, Mr. Gladstone's government stood firm against any suggestion that they should support a modification in the Greek Constitution. Braila exposed to Clarendon, and Vyzantios exposed to Europe, the flaws and follies of the prevailing system. King George confessed to Elliot that without some reforms he did not see how he could continue on the throne. But Elliot, as Lord Russell's brother-in-law would not, and as Gladstone's representative could not, lend countenance to any such proposals. This attitude was consistently maintained. On 1 May 1871 Lord Granville penned a long instruction to the newly appointed minister at Athens, Mr. Stuart. In this, he admitted that the English government still entertained a strong impression that those persons directly responsible for the Dilessi affair had not been touched by the Enquiry. But he added that if, as was not improbable, King George were to speak to Stuart as he had spoken twelve months earlier to Elliot, Stuart was to give His Majesty no encouragement whatever.[1] The event proved the wisdom of this course. Gradually, with many crises and backslidings, a better system of democracy was established. The distraught youth of 1870, who felt he should never hold up his head again, and who many times thought of abandoning the country of his adoption, yet remained on its throne during the next forty-three years, and

[1] Granville to Stuart, 1 May 1871.

lived to see it prosperous and victorious before the assassin's bullet put an end to his life of brilliant achievement and devotion. His early troubles were all forgotten, even his terrible feud with Mr. Koumoundouros. And when Koumoundouros died in 1883, he was so affectionately regarded by the throne that King George afterwards told his children, 'how he had loved this old statesman, who had always been full of consideration for him and had never caused him a moment's anxiety or pain'![1]

The Russian policy of exploiting the Dilessi imbroglio to the detriment of English influence in Greece received a rude check from the sudden and total collapse of France and the emergence of Prussia as a power of the first magnitude. The Russian government had seized the occasion to emancipate their country from the provisions of the Black Sea Treaty of 1856. But the writing was on the wall. By the summer of 1871 they were beginning to think that a rapprochement with England, at least in the Near East, might be a prudent course. One of the curses of the Greek kingdom since its foundation had been that the three Protecting Powers – England, France and Russia – had continually followed separate and often conflicting policies in regard to it. Now, in June 1871, Novikow's successor, Sabourow, called on Mr. Stuart and proposed, in a most conciliatory manner, that the two of them should in future agree to work in harmony. Stuart accepted this proposal with relief: the more so, since King George, doubtless on Sabourow's advice, had recently said to him that 'great good might arise if Greek politicians could once for all be convinced that Great Britain and Russia were not supporting or encouraging separate parties or pursuing conflicting objects in this country.'[2]

As for Mr. Noel, he had learnt his lesson. After a long holiday in England he returned in 1872 to Achmetaga. But he resolutely abstained from any interference in the local politics of

[1] Prince Nicholas, 29.
[2] Stuart to Granville, 9 June, 1871.

the island. This, to be sure, did not prevent an attempt to assas-
sinate him during the elections of 1873. But he survived; and,
gradually and perseveringly, made his peace with all around
him. Perhaps the most satisfactory aftermath of the Dilessi
tragedy is to be found in an idyllic description of a visit made
to Achmetaga by Hans Müller in 1881.[1] On his arrival Müller
was received, with that splendid hospitality for which the mansion has always been celebrated, by Mrs. Frank Noel and her
sister, the blonde, blue-eyed Miss Ada, who seemed to him 'a
good fairy sent from heaven'. He stayed a week, and compared
his visit to a sojourn among the lotus-eaters. Frank Noel was
absent; he was on a visit to his friend and neighbour Mr.
Tombazis. But he soon returned and, on Müller's departure,
offered him an introduction to another friend at Chalkis, Mr.
Basil Boudouris.

Far different was the fate of Colonel Theagenis and Mr.
Erskine. Both had committed errors, but their punishment was
out of proportion to their blunderings. Theagenis indeed had
been less than candid in his accounts of his own conduct. He
had undertaken his mission to Oropós with only the slender-
est hopes of liberating the prisoners, and had been too ready to
terminate his negotiation with Takos. After the disaster he stated that he had spent 'all day', 'several hours', and, elsewhere,
'seven hours' in argument with the chiefs. But Noel, who had
been present, declared that the Colonel had stayed no more
than an hour, and at last Theagenis himself corrected his estimate to two. Again, he denied that he had known the contents
of Erskine's guarantee of 14 April, although in fact Noel had,
at Takos' request, read it out to him. Noel and Finlay assailed
him without mercy: 'the most unfit for a purpose of this kind,
I should say, that could be found in the whole kingdom', said
Noel, and Finlay added, 'This opinion of his unfitness is general

[1] H. Müller, *Griechische Reisen und Studien* (Leipzig, 1887), 124–9.

in Athens.'[1] In a private letter to Alice Noel,[2] Finlay went further still: 'Had that fool Colonel Theagenes not gone to Oropós at all, I feel convinced Frank would have terminated the business favourably. Colonel Theagenes is only a grammatikos [3] with the rank of colonel, and no soldier . . . I believe now that he is a well-disposed person, but utterly destitute of clear judgment and tact.' His English friends, Church, Gladstone, Baillie-Cochrane, Miss Wyse, tried to stand up for him; but their excuses were scouted in the Commons by Sir Henry Bulwer, who, not content with having called Theagenis an assassin in the debate of 20 May, overwhelmed him once more with sarcasm and vituperation in the resumed discussion of 2 August. That he should so suffer at the hands of the fellow-countrymen of Edward Lear and Richard Church was indescribably painful to him. 'No one of course likes those who treat him with unkindness,' he said sadly to Finlay. He retired to his property at Thebes. Two years later, he was dead.

Mr. Erskine's career was in ruins. To be dismissed from the Foreign Service was nearly impossible; but he was one upon whom failure had set its ineffaceable stamp. He wrote repeatedly to Granville requesting extensions of his leave of absence—for two months, for another six, for yet another three. He pretended that he should return to Athens when his health was restored; but this was not to be thought of. At length, in 1872, a post was found for him at the other end of Europe, in Stockholm. Here he lingered obscurely during nine years. He died in 1883. With all his faults and weaknesses, he was more to be pitied than blamed. He was, it is true, shockingly ignorant of Greece, and hence unfit for his post. But he was, like his contemporaries, caught between two sharply distinct eras of English diplomacy. With reasonable luck, he would have got by. As it was, luck

---

[1] Noel, *Letters*, 27.
[2] Finlay to Alice Noel, 25 May 1870 (N.-B.).
[3] As we should say — a pen-pusher.

turned against him. The single, sudden crisis came upon him, and he had neither wisdom nor strength to confront it.[1]

Alexander Anemoyiannis, for all his gloomy apprehensions and his tarnished reputation, did somehow manage to re-establish himself, and continued during many years to conduct the more confident or more careless of foreign tourists over the countryside. He was fortunate in avoiding the uncoveted 'black bean' of John Murray, whose Handbook of 1872 cleared him of all blame. English travellers, perhaps understandably, fought shy of him;[2] but Agnes Smith came across him in 1883, in charge of a party of Americans and prudently escorted by a posse of militiamen.[3]

The brigand Karavidas, who had been taken in Turkey, was extradited to Greece and beheaded. The brigand Lioris had been offered a pardon if he would produce evidence of value in unravelling the mystery; and he had responded with testimony against Thanopoulos, Basil Boudouris and the shepherd Goggos. The Greek Enquiry rejected his allegations against the two former, but accepted it against Goggos. However, at the trial of Goggos, Lioris altogether withdrew his evidence, and maintained that, at his interrogations, he had been depressed, drunk, wounded and, in short, not responsible for his own words. Was he then to be reprieved? Cookson was so much disgusted with him that he declined to move in the matter at all. But Granville, after consulting the Lord Chancellor, thought he should be pardoned, and Stuart was instructed to put in a word for him.

Brigandage, as Cookson had predicted, seemed scarcely to have been diminished by the well-meaning attempts of Deligeorgis and Koumoundouros. In 1872 it seemed to be as prevalent as ever; and the dictum of Sir Charles Trevelyan that 'the

[1] Rumbold, I, 144.
[2] R. R. Farrer, *A Tour in Greece* (London, 1882), 72.
[3] Smith, 349.

knell of brigandage was rung at Pikermes' was, to say the least of it, premature. But in September 1873 it received a check. Takos Arvanitákis, driven across the Turkish border into Greece, was shot and killed by Greek troops near Lamia. So disappeared the last surviving member of the band who was capable of telling the whole truth of Dilessi, of the messengers who had come to him on the night of 14 April, and of the mysterious letter brought to him on 19 April by the hand of his brother George Yannou.

In the baffling labyrinths of the Enquiry, and in the murky twilight of international intrigue, we seem to have strayed far from the protagonists in that hideous drama, the four who lay dead on the Boeotian coast. But 'the old fire of the English character', which seemed to Lord Carnarvon to have 'burnt out like straw', was not yet so cold that England could refuse to honour with due dignity and decorum the homecoming of her dead children. For Herbert and Vyner were after all not to rest in the country where they had met so cruel a fate: and this was as Herbert at least would have wished. A few months before the disaster the American minister, Charles Tuckerman, had met his young friend Herbert walking with a very long face. Herbert explained that he had been visiting the Protestant Cemetery near the Ilissos, and that it had depressed his spirits. 'I don't half like the look-out of that place,' he told Tuckerman; 'I shouldn't like to lie there.' And then, with a strange prescience, he added, 'I shall tell Erskine to send me home.'

In the event, he lay there twenty-four hours only. After his interment on 23 April came instructions from Highclere and Gautby that he and Vyner were to be sent home. Herbert was exhumed. Both bodies were embalmed and set on board H.M.S. *Antelope*. At Malta the coffins were transferred to the steamship *Delta*, which sailed at once for England. At three o'clock on the afternoon of Saturday, 14 May, *Delta* passed between Hurst Castle and the Island. Flags on all shipping in the Solent and Southampton Water were lowered to half-mast. Two hours later the vessel put in to Southampton Roads. The whole city was in mourning. Shops were shut. Men and women put on black. The transfer of the coffins from ship to shore, and their slow progress to the railway station, were carried out in a solemn silence, broken only by the muffled peals which rang from the steeples and by the intermittent roar of the minute-guns on the Battery Platform. On the following morning, in Westminster Abbey, the sermon was preached by the Dean, Arthur Stanley, who himself, ten years before, had stood upon the summit of Mount Pentelicus with Sir Thomas Wyse and Alexander Anemoyiannis. He dwelt on the sudden and inexplicable nature of the event, for which their only comfort lay in a resort to the wider perspective embraced by the writer of the seventy-seventh Psalm. He pictured the three historic nations, England and Italy and Greece, bowed in sorrow over the biers. He drew consolation from the circumstance that his countrymen, harassed and tormented, and with the world's eye upon them, had done nothing to compromise the traditions of courage and honour and faith in which an Englishman should die. And lastly he reminded his hearers that, even in that shadowy valley, there had been One at hand to counsel and to sustain: 'Their souls', he said, 'are with Him who gave them. The way was dark and terrible. The footsteps of the merciful God were hard to trace. Yet through the deep waters He led them, we may humbly hope, to the haven where they would be . . . He led them to the long, last home, where there shall be no more parting, and where the former things are passed away.'

# APPENDIX

PRO F.O. 32/406 No: 207

Mr. Erskine to Earl Granville, 12 July 1870.

Confidential.

...But although M. Zaïmis is either unwilling or unable to comply with the demand for information as to the internal condition of Greece made to him by Her Majesty's Government, I have fortunately found M. Valaority less reticent in this respect: he has placed in my hands, confidentially, for communication to Your Lordship a Memorandum of which the enclosed is a translation, and which appears to me to describe in no exaggerated terms the effects which have been caused by a long course of brigandage and misrule.

Should Your Lordship have occasion to publish the contents of this document, M. Valaority requests me to say that, for obvious reasons, he hopes no mention will be made of his name, and that any direct charge of complicity with brigandage on the part of the principal political personages in this country may be suppressed.

It is notorious to those who have lived long in Greece that most of her leading men have recourse to such practices to support or increase their political influence, but it is difficult to establish a charge of this nature by direct evidence, and at all events M. Valaority does not wish to involve himself uselessly in such a controversy as that which has recently been provoked by the publication in England of a statement made to me by M. Zaïmis to the same effect.

[Enclosure]
Confidential. Athens, July 1, 1870.
Translation.

193

## MEMORANDUM

Irregular government, which prevailed in Greece ever since the date of its independence, has become gradually worse since the interregnum, and has reduced the country to a deplorable condition.

Nomarchs, Eparchs, Treasurers, Ephors, Collectors of Customs, Officers of the Gendarmerie, in fact almost all the administrators and public servants and, still worse, the dispensers of justice, are chiefly or wholly concerned in trying to please the influential men of the provinces and thus purchase, by the audacious violation of law and at the cost of injury of the public interests, their own continuance in office.

Hence the cruel persecution, in certain localities, of enemies of influential men, who owe money to the state: absurd comdemnations: acquittal of criminals: scandalous pardons of condemned brigands and assassins: the pillage of the public revenue: the concession of national lands: partial oppression of the inhabitants by the detachments from flying columns: and, finally, calling into life brigands and outlaws in order to perpetuate the existing bad government of the kingdom.

The question which now occupies attention is not so much that of the general affairs of the kingdom, as that of public security, which has recently been shown to be so defective that, if general serious measures be not taken for ensuring the eradication of the evil, Greece will in time to come demand the compassion, whilst she draws down the indignation, of the civilized world.

As to this subject of security, without going back to former times to prove by facts the pitiful state of the country, it will suffice to take into consideration the acts of brigandage committed within a short period (say from 1869 and onwards), and we shall quickly form an idea of the calamities inflicted on the inhabitants of most of the provinces of the kingdom.

It is not to be supposed that the following list comprises all the horrible crimes which since the beginning of 1869 have been committed in Greece by brigands and outlaws, as it is not easy to gather quite comprehensive details respecting them.

[109 instances of banditry are next listed: they include more than fifty murders, two of them by torture, many other examples of torture and mutilation, and two cases of violation of women, a crime very unusual among brigands, who regarded it as unlucky.]

After the recital of the criminal acts committed by brigands and outlaws from 1869 and since, it is natural to inquire into the reasons why so many malefactors exist in Greece.

One of the first causes is the raising of many bodies of armed men who at various times have been worked upon and made use of by different politicians under the pretext of conquering some portion of the Turkish Empire;

Intentional indifference on the part of those competent to put a stop to the harangues of the promoters of the 'Grande idée', and so save their victims, who deliver themselves up to a life of brigandage;

The inefficiency of the garrison on the frontier;

The laxity shown by the neighbouring state in the pursuit of those criminals who take refuge there; and

The protection afforded to brigands and outlaws by statesmen who create and maintain their influence by means of the gun and the knife.

In now developing the last of these causes, and without referring to a time further back than that of the so-called Parliamentary Government – that is to say, from the period when the country was under the worst government – we may state facts known to everyone and sufficiently palpable to convince the most sceptical person that the Greek Nation would prosper under the New Dynasty were prudent, patriotic and incorruptible men to be called upon at any cost to assume the government of the country.

In June 1863 M. Bulgaris was not at the head of affairs. This circumstance forced reflection upon him, in consequence of which the brigand chief Kyriakos Melissoras was invited at the head of several turbulent men and ex-brigands to the capital of the kingdom. Athens became a scene of slaughter and desolation and the government fell into the hands of the friends of the above-mentioned politician.

The brigand chief was not considered by the then government as acting criminally; on the contrary, he represented the character of a patriot, and was proclaimed (in derision of the champions of 1821, who were dying from hunger) a pensioner. He receives his pay up to this day from the Treasury, and was acquitted through the efforts of his political protector, when tried on the accusation of having robbed in Athens the house of M. Lascarides.

Another brigand chief called Kyriakos Kappasis was appointed by M. Coumoundouros, towards the end of the year 1866, chief of the brigands and outlaws of Phthiotis. He disturbed order in the Turkish provinces with the sole view of helping the return of his political protector to power, and in recompense was granted a pension from the public treasury, which he continues to receive.

Is it denied that M. Coumoundouros whilst premier sent 150 brigands, the body-guards of several of his political friends, to Crete?

Everyone knows that there once existed in Attica a brigand chief Kitzo: this person has been succeeded by the brigand chief Spanos. The protector of this man has been asserted by the inhabitants of the capital to be Major-General Soutzo, who is still the deputy for Attica. His numerous partisans maintain that this reproach is unjust. But when one considers that this gentleman, like other statesmen, exercises his provincial influence through brigands and outlaws; that in 1864, during the

premiership of M. Bulgaris, the Procureur du Roi, M. J. Nico-
laides, demanded permission to imprison the said Soutzo, who
was accused of sheltering brigands, but did not obtain it; that
the brother of the brigand chief Kitzo, the brigand Piliou, and
two other brigands, were taken by the gendarmerie from his
house and sent to Crete via the Piraeus and Syra; that previously to the death of Kitzo, and since, under the rule of Spanos,
only such of the inhabitants of Attica as differed with M. Soutzo were ill-treated by the brigands; that hardly any of the com-
manders of the flying columns dared to attack or pursue brigands in Attica; that, if any one of them, as for instance Captain
Liacopoulos, had tried to do his duty, he would either have
been recalled or punished; that not only were the sergeants of
the gendarmeríe, Poulou and Korasea, who had left the Arvanitei unmolested in Megaris, not punished but on the contrary
allowed to serve in Attica; that the brigands in Acarnania were
promised an ignominious truce, immediately after his arrival
there as Minister of War; and lastly that he never took steps to
pursue the brigands in Attica and Boeotia who were there
some months and thus caused the animadversions on other
statesmen after the recent terrible act of brigandage; from all
this it is not surprising that the public should call M. Soutzo a
brigand chief, and easily accounts for his having assured the
English minister that 'the brigands were not worse than other
men who were considered honest.'

It cannot too be doubted that M. Bulgaris' and M.
Coumoundouros' political friends in the provinces protect
brigands and outlaws.

At Vonitza, for example, brigands are protected by the
deputy D. Grivas, the ex-deputy Athanasius Monasteriotis and
the brothers Tzelio. At Naupactie by the deputies E. Plastira and
N. Pharmaki. At Valto by the deputy J. Karayanopoulos and the
ex-deputy Strato. At Phthiotis by the deputies Diovouniotis
and Zouloumis, the father-in-law of the deputy Tsirimokou,

Major-General Kautoyanni and Colonel Balatsos. At Chalcis by the deputies Grizioti and Averoff and by the ex-deputy Boudouris. At Thebes by the friends of Lieutenant-General S. Milio. At Livadea [by] the friend of the said general, the demarch Koutzopetalos. At Trichomia by Colonel Scaltza. At Megaris by the deputy Malea and his relations. At Corinth by the deputies Messrs. Notara and Joannin Delyanni. At Elis by the friends of the deputies Messrs. Chrestenites.

At Messenia the outlaws are protected by the deputies Pyrroti and Boutos. At Pylos by the deputy Mysirlis. At Tryphilia by the unpunished incendiary of the capital of this province, the deputy Grigoriades. At Gortynia by the friends of the Minister of Finance, Theodore Delyanni, the deputies Regopoulos and Roilos, the lawyer Eutaxiopoulos, the demarch of Cheniades and the friend and son–in–law of B. Nicolopoulo, Monsieur Spirakopoulos ex-demarch of Caritena.

The brigands and outlaws are protected by statesmen, of which fact official evidence may be found in the archives of the Legislative Body.

During the election of 1869 all the local newspapers were filled with recriminations; it was stated for instance that in several of the provinces of Continental Greece, of the Peloponesus and of Euboea, the elections had been carried by means of brigands and outlaws. At first the statements in the newspapers were considered exaggerations, but when in the Office of the Chamber of Deputies signed petitions were deposited which gave the true history of what had taken place at the elections, no doubt remained that brigands and outlaws had been present at them and by threats and violence had secured the election of their protectors.

There are other facts which prove that brigands are protected by the principal deputies and demarchs. For example, at Corinth the deputies Notara sheltered brigands and were denounced on this account; but who would believe that M.

Coumoundouros left no stone unturned to clear away this accusation from his friends? Or that M. Bulgaris, in the hope of gaining the said parties, dared in 1868 formally to assure H.M. the King that MM. Notara had not committed the said crime imputed to them?

To the deputy Pharmaki they lately wrote from Naupactie that his friends had killed four brigand chiefs who had interfered to their prejudice in the late municipal elections. Meanwhile no judicial authority has made an effort to discover those who had invited the brigands to interfere in the elections.

Tzelios, the candidate for the mayorhood of Astakos, assured in writing the Commandant de Place there that he could deliver into the hands of the authorities a certain band of brigands, provided that the order issued for his arrest were suspended, he having been accused of sheltering brigands. Nevertheless, he was seen a few days back freely going about the streets of Athens, and the brigands have never been delivered up to the authorities.

Friends of the deputies Chrestenites, demarchs, were imprisoned for complicity with the band of brigands of Magira in the capture of M. Valsimachi. Meanwhile MM. Chrestenites spare no means to save from justice the brigand-sheltering demarchs.

The friend of M. Bulgaris, the deputy Zouloumi, lies under heavy suspicion of having sheltered brigands. Has any enquiry been made into this? None.

The deputy of Megaris, Maléa, and his brother the ex-mayor of Edyllion are in prison, accused of having sheltered the Arvanitei; can anyone be sure they will not go unpunished since all of the same party are for them? M. Coumoundouros and General Milio have had recourse to every measure to clear them.

The demarch of Livadea, Koutzopetalos, was indicted before the Court of Assize for having sheltered brigands.

Notwithstanding this, not only has he not been arrested, though for some months past concealed in Athens, but he has succeeded through the efforts of MM. Bulgaris and Milio in obtaining a decree from the 'Cour Royale' that proceedings against him should provisionally be suspended.

At Patras the brigand Gazetta was arrested whilst following Lieutenant-Colonel Scaltza. Nothing was done to him. M. Botzaris, an officer of the army, accused the deputy Plastira of harbouring brigands. Has anything been done on the part of justice to certify the crime? The father of this officer, Lieutenant-Colonel Demi Noti Botzaris, stated that in his hands he had letters of Plastira in which he, Plastira, begged him to suspend the pursuit in Naupactie of the brigands his friends. Has any enquiry taken place about this?

The deputies Griziotis and Averoff and the ex-deputy Boudouris, as well as Mr. Noel the friend of the second, are considered by the public to have caused the recent murders. Will justice take account of this? Probably not.

In face of these, surely every doubt will be removed that the atrocious murder of foreigners is the fruit of the protection which criminals find in Greek statesmen – very often from those who are in power, as happened in 1868, when the then premier, M. Bulgaris, protected the Director of Police and police officers, who, in the very capital of the kingdom, robbed certain Greek citizens who had arrived from Alexandria.

Endorsed [by Mr. Hammond]
    Better not print.
                            For  The Queen
                                 Mr. Gladstone
                                 Circulate

# BIBLIOGRAPHY

(ITEMS MARKED WITH AN ASTERISK
ARE IN THE GREEK LANGUAGE)

I.      About, E., *La Grèce contemporaine,* Paris, 1854; English translation, *Greece and the Greeks of the Present Day,* Edinburgh, 1855.

2.      About, E., *Le Roi des montagnes,* Paris, 1857.

3.      Anon. (see Gennadios, J.)

4.      Anon., 'Marathon and its Brigands', *Cornhill Magazine,* no.126, 1870.

5★      Anon., *Those responsible for the existence of brigandage in Peloponnese,* Tripolis, 1870.

6.★      Arniotákis, E, *The Voice of Greece,* Smyrna, 1871.

7.★      Aspréas, G. K., *Political History of Modern Greece,* II, Athens, 1923.

8.      Austrian Dispatches, Athens-Vienna (Haymerle to Beust) 26 February-25 June 1870: Haus-, Hof- und Staatsarchiv Wien, Polit. Archiv XVI, Griechenland, Berichte 1870, Kart. 28.

9.      *Blackwood's Edinburgh Magazine,* no. 658, August 1870, 'Our own Commissioner's Report.'

10.      Burnouf, E., *Le brigandage en Grèce, Revue des deux mondes* 87, 1870, 987-1009.

11.      Deschamps, G., *La Grèce d'aujourd'hui,* new ed., Paris, 1901.

12.      Finlay, G., *A History of Greece . . . to 1864* (ed. Tozer), VII, Oxford, 1877.

13.      Finlay, G., 'Affairs of Greece, 1869-1873' (AG): being manuscript drafts of articles to *The Times* and of private letters to its editors Mowbray Morris and John C. MacDonald, now in the possession of the British

School of Archaeology at Athens.

14. Finlay, G., Letters (N.-B.): being unpublished letters from George Finlay to Edward and Alice Noel, 1870-1871, now in the possession of the Rt. Hon. Philip J. Noel-Baker, P.C., M.P.

15. Foreign Office Dispatches, Athens-London, London-Athens, 1870-1871; Public Record Office, F.O., 32 vols. 402-419 (Chancery Lane), F.O. 286 vols. 265-276 (Ashridge).

16. (Gennadios, J.), *Notes on the Recent Murders by Brigands in Greece*, London, 1870.

17. Gladstone Papers, British Museum MSS., Add. 44134, ff. 186-216; 44638, ff. 67-121.

18.★ (Greek) Foreign Ministry, *Documents on the act of brigandage*, Athens, 1871.

19.★ Greek newspapers, 1870: *Aión, Ethnikon Pnevma, Ethnophylax, La Grèce* (in French), *Mellon, Merimna, Palingenesia, Proïnos Kiryx.*

20. Grenier, A., *La Grèce en 1863*, Paris, 1863.

21. *Handbook for Travellers in Greece*, London, John Murray, 1872.

22. Höeg, C., *Les Saracatsans,* 2 vols., Paris and Copenhagen, 1925.

23.★ Koronaios, P., *Reflexions on the establishment of order and the causes preventing it*, Athens, 1869.

24.★ Kyriakidis, E. K., *History of Contemporary Hellenism*, II, Athens, 1892.

25. LHéritier, M., (Driault et LHéritier), *Histoire diplomatique de la Grèce de 1821 à nos jours*, III, Paris, 1925.

26.★ Milisis, G., Two speeches of G.M., Deputy of Hermionis, Athens, 1871.

27.★ Moschonisios, A., *The mirror of brigandage in Greece*, Hermoupolis, 1869.

28. Nicholas of Greece, H.R.H. Prince, *My Fifty Years*, 2nd

ed., London, n.d. (?1927).

29.   Noel, F. E. (Frank), *Letters of Mr. Frank Noel respecting the Murder by Brigands of the Captives of Marathon and his Prosecution by the Greek Government.* With an Intro duction by his Father, London and Edinburgh, 1871. (George Finlay's copy of this publication, now in the possession of the British School of Archaeology at Athens, has Finlay's MS. notes in the margins.)

30★ Noel, F. E., *Memorandum of Mr. Frank Noel to the Appeal Court in Athens against Resolution no. 1028 of the Athens Chambre des mises en accusation,* Athens, 1871.

31★ Noel, F. E., *Special Memorandum of Mr. Frank Noel refuting the views of Resolution no. 1028 of the Athens Chambre des mises en accusation, in the order followed by the latter,* Athens, 1871.

32.★   *Official Report of the Trial* of those accused, 19 April (= 1 May n.s.), Athens, 1871. (The copy seen by me bears no title: I have therefore called it the *Official Report of the Trial.*)

33★ *Resolution of the Chambre de mises en accusation of Athens, no. 1028,* Athens, November 1870.

34.   Rumbold, H., *Recollections of a Diplomatist,* 2 vols., London, 1902; *Final Recollections,* London, 1905.

35.   Senior, N. W., *A Journal Kept in Turkey and Greece,* London, 1859.

36.   Smith, A., *Glimpses of Greek Life and Scenery,* London, 1884.

37.★   Sotiropoulos, S., *Thirty-six days of Captivity and Consort with Brigands,* 2nd ed., Athens, 1867; English version, Bagdon, J. O., *The Brigands of the Morea,* 2 vols., London, 1868.

38.   Townshend, F. T., *A Cruise in Greek Waters,* London, 1870.

39.   Tuckerman, C. K., *The Greeks of Today,* 2nd ed., New

York, 1878.
40.*     Vyzantios, A. S., *Works*, ed. G.S.V., Athens, 1902.
41.     Watbled, E., *Les brigands de Marathon*, Tours, 1897.
42.     Wyse, T., *Impressions of Greece*, London, 1871.
43.     Xenos, S., *East and West*, London, 1865.

# INDEX

Other books in this series are listed below. Copies should be available from your local bookshop but in the case of difficulty can be purchased direct from the publisher.

**Prion Books Limited**, Unit L, 32-34 Gordon House Road, London NW5 ILP

The Atrocities of the Pirates
by **Aaron Smith**                          £8.99.........copies
The Marquis of Montrose
by **John Buchan**                          £8.99.........copies
Napoleon and his Marshals
by **A.G. Macdonell**                       £8.99.........copies
The River War
by **Winston S. Churchill**                 £9.99.........copies
Napoleons Letter's
by **J.M.Thompson**                         £10.00.........copies
Disraeli
by **Robert Blake**                         £16.00.........copies

Payments can be made by cheque or postal order (payable to Prion Books Ltd).
Unfortunately we cannot accept credit cards.
Do not send cash or currency. UK customers and B.F.P.O. please allow £1.00 for postage and packing for the first book, plus 50p for each additional book. Overseas customers including Ireland, please allow £2.00 for the first book plus £1.00 for the second book. **Orders for three or more books placed at the same time are supplied post free**.

NAME (Block Letters)
ADDRESS


I enclose my remittance for £